/17

EVANGELICAL CONVERSION
IN GREAT BRITAIN 1516–1695

By the same Author

The History of Ridley Hall, Cambridge
Volume 1 (1941)

A History of the Parish Church of
St. Mary, Truro, Cornwall (1948)

A History of the 'Church-in-the-Wood',
Hollington, Sussex   (1949)

A History of the Parish Church of
St. Helen, Ore, Sussex (1951)

The History of Ridley Hall, Cambridge
Volume 2 (1953)

A History of Training for the Ministry
of the Church of England, 1800--1874 (1955)

Evangelical Conversion in Great Britain,
1696–1845 (1959)

Voluntary Religious Societies,
1520–1799 (1963)

F. W. B. BULLOCK

Ph.D., D.D.

Canon Emeritus of Truro Cathedral

EVANGELICAL CONVERSION IN GREAT BRITAIN 1516-1695

BUDD & GILLATT   *   ST. LEONARDS ON SEA

Published 1966

Printed by
Budd & Gillatt
North Street
St. Leonards-on-Sea
Sussex

CONTENTS

PREFACE

IN MY book, *Evangelical Conversion in Great Britain,* 1696 – 1845, published in 1959, the experiences of thirty people, who passed through a conversion crisis during that period and within that geographical area, were recorded and described. Those thirty narratives, arranged in order by the dates of their conversions, covering the span of 150 years, gave an average of one instance for every five years, but were not of course evenly spaced, some examples falling close together, while others were more widely dispersed. There were twelve between 1696 and 1745, twelve between 1746 and 1795, and six between 1796 and 1845.

In this present book, there are the same territorial limits, but the time is earlier – from 1516 to 1695, a span of 180 years. The average of one instance for every five years is maintained, for the number of narratives is thirty-six. Their spacing is naturally uneven, there being ten between 1516 and 1575, sixteen between 1576 and 1635, and ten between 1636 and 1695.

Among the thirty-six stories no example has been included between 1681 and 1695 inclusive, but an impressive though very brief one, dating from 1695, may be included as an extra here, both for its own interest and as a link between the 1516 – 1695 volume and that of 1696 – 1845. John Wesley says in his *Journal* on September 14, 1751, that on that day he preached at St. Lawrence, near Bodmin:—'I found God was there, even before I opened my mouth, to a small, loving, congregation; one of whom had been sensible of his acceptance with God for above six and fifty years'.[1] This carries back precisely to the year 1695. It is a particularly good example of the lasting nature of a conversion, which must have taken place fairly early in life.

As with the thirty of the later period, so with the thirty-six now recorded, the narratives are given whenever possible in the words of the actual experients, together with their opinions if available about their own conversions and (mostly in the section on doctrinal belief) about the subject of conversion in general. These stories concentrate upon the conversion experiences of the individuals concerned; they are not biographies, but a few biographical details, especially of the less well-known people, are added in order to provide a little background and clarify the situation.

A few of these thirty-six accounts of conversions are extremely familiar, e.g. those of Bunyan and Fox, but most of them are not readily accessible outside very large libraries. All but six of their subjects are indeed included, sometimes at considerable length, in the *Dictionary of National Biography*,[2] but the full records of their conversion experiences could not be related there. So it is hoped that the grouping together in this present volume of the many personal narratives of that experience may be of use. Each one is an intensely human story, while the whole series gives a notable testimony to the manifold workings of the Spirit of God.

[1]Ed. N. Curnock, *The Journal of the Reverend John Wesley*. Standard Edition (1909), Vol. 3, p. 538.
[2]The exceptions are David Straiton, Richard Rothwell, John Gifford, Sarah Howley, Thomas Tregosse, and Sir Alan Broderick.

The succeeding discussion is certainly much less valuable, but may yet be of some interest. The same divisions as those in the previous book have been retained—'Psychology and the Conversion Experience', with four sub-divisions, and 'The Relation of the Conversion Experience . . . to Doctrinal Belief', but the many references to and quotations from the works of psychologists and others have not been repeated, nor has it been thought necessary to discuss again the question of 'The Validity of the Experience of Conversion'. This volume should therefore be regarded as supplementary to the earlier volume, which it is hoped may be read first. Like its predecessor, this work ends with a section on 'The Value of the Experience of Conversion'.

It is not surprising, but it is a great pity that more information has not survived about the religious experiences of those who met at the White Horse Inn at Cambridge or at Cardinal College, Oxford, where they discussed the teaching of the New Testament and the works of Luther, and it is most unfortunate that William Tyndale did not record the details of his own early spiritual development; one would also like to know how George Stafford, Nicholas Ridley, George Wishart, and many others came to find their way; but the experiences of those here recorded give the clue. Among those of later date, who experienced conversions of a notable sort, we might add Henry Barrowe, a lawyer and Cambridge graduate, converted suddenly from a profligate life on hearing a sermon about 1580;[1] 'Mr. Price, who from open profligacy and vice' had, about 1615, 'an extraordinary conversion' in Cambridge, where it was talked about freely, and who

[1] D.N.B.

became a minister at King's Lynn[1]— apparently Nicholas Price, Fellow of Magdalene College,[2] preacher at St. Nicholas', King's Lynn;[3] Oliver Cromwell, converted about 1628;[4] James Ley, third Earl of Marlborough, 'a contemner of religion', who was 'brought to a different sense of things upon real conviction, even in full health'[5] about 1664; and Margaret Charlton, who had delighted in 'pride, vanity, and romances', but was converted about 1660 and later married Richard Baxter.[6]

[1]T. Goodwin, Works, Vol 2 (1861), pp, xxi, lix.   [2]Alumni Cantabrigienses.
[3]H. J. Hillen, History of the Borough of King's Lynn (1907), Vol. 1, p. 414.
[4]J. L. Sandford, Studies and Illustrations of the Great Rebellion (1858), pp. 210–226; T. Carlyle, ed. S. C. Lomas, The Letters and Speeches of Oliver Cromwell (1904), Vol. 1, pp. 89–92; R. S. Paul, The Lord Protector (1955), pp. 35–42.
[5]The Two Noble Converts (1680); J. Tillotson, Works (1752), Vol 1, p. xxi, footnote 1.
[6]Ed. S. Clarke, The Lives of Sundry Eminent Persons (1683), Part 2, pp. 181–182.

THOMAS BILNEY c. 1495 – 1531

Conversion c. 1516

THOMAS BILNEY was born probably about 1495; he
was ordained priest at Ely in 1519; he became a
Bachelor of Canon Law and a Fellow of Trinity Hall,
Cambridge, in 1520 – 21.[1]

It was in a letter written in 1527 to Cuthbert Tunstall,
Bishop of London, that Bilney gave a clear account of
the conversion which he had experienced roughly a
decade previously:—' . . . at last I heard speak of Jesus,
even then when the New Testament was first set forth
by Erasmus; which when I understood to be eloquently
done by him, being allured rather by the Latin than by
the word of God (for at that time I knew not what it
meant), I bought even by the providence of God, as I
do now well understand and perceive; and at the first
reading (as I well remember) I chanced upon this
sentence of St. Paul (O most sweet and comfortable
sentence to my soul) in 1 Tim. i, "It is a true saying, and
worthy of all men to be embraced, that Christ Jesus
came into the world to save sinners; of whom I am the
chief and principal". This one sentence, through God's
instruction and inward working, which I did not then
perceive, did so exhilarate my heart, being before
wounded with the guilt of my sins, and being almost in
despair, that immediately I felt a marvellous comfort
and quietness, insomuch "that my bruised bones
leaped for joy."

After this, the scripture began to be more pleasant

---

[1]*Alumni Cantabrigienses*; *Dictionary of National Biography.*

unto me than the honey or the honey-comb;[1] wherein I learned, that all my travails, all my fasting and watching, all the redemption of masses and pardons, being done without trust in Christ, who only saveth his people from their sins; these, I say, I learned to be nothing else but even (as St. Augustine saith) a hasty and swift running out of the right way . . .

As soon as (according to the measure of grace given unto me of God) I began to taste and savour of this heavenly lesson, which no man can teach but only God, who revealed the same unto Peter, I desired the Lord to increase my faith; and at last I desired nothing more, than that I, being so comforted by him, might be strengthened by his Holy Spirit and grace from above, that I might teach the wicked his ways, which are mercy and truth; and that the wicked might be converted unto him by me, who sometime was also wicked . . .'[2]

Bilney did in fact convert many, including Sir William Paget, Thomas Arthur and Hugh Latimer,[3] also (with the assistance of Arthur, Stafford and others) Dr. Robert Barnes[4], and (with Arthur) John Lambert.[5] Matthew Parker regarded Bilney as his 'spiritual master'.[6]

Erasmus was in Cambridge as the Lady Margaret Professor of Divinity from 1511 to 1513. His first edition of the New Testament in Greek (March, 1516) was entitled *Novum Instrumentum*; it included also a

---

[1]*Cf.* Psalm xix. 10.
[2]Letter quoted in J. Foxe, *Acts and Monuments* (1877 edition), Vol 4, pp. 635-636.
[3]*Ibid.*, p. 620; A. Gray, *Cambridge University, An Episodical History* (1926), pp. 133-135.
[4]Barnes took his D.D. degree at Cambridge in 1523, and was converted in 1524 or 1525—*ibid.*, p. 620; *Dictionary of National Biography*.
[5]Foxe, Vol. 4, p. 620; *cf.* also, Vol. 5, p. 181.　　[6]Gray, *op. cit.*, p. 134.

Latin translation (which particularly appealed to Bilney), short notes, and three introductory sections.[1] A second edition (1519) followed, in which the title was altered to *Novum Testamentum*. This has made some writers think that Bilney read the later edition and that his conversion could not have been before 1519;[2] but Bilney's own phrase, 'was first set forth by Erasmus', implies that it was a copy of the 1516 edition which he bought and eagerly studied.[3]

Bilney was burned at the stake for his faith in 1531 at Norwich.

[1]J. H. Kurtz, *Church History*, transl. J. Macpherson, Vol. 2 (1889), p. 225.
[2]M. L. Loane, *Masters of the English Reformation* (1954), pp. 2–8.
[3]Cf. H. C. Porter, *Reformation and Reaction in Tudor Cambridge* (1958), pp. 35–40.

2

JOHN FRITH 1503 – 1533

Conversion c.1523

JOHN FRITH, born at Westerham in Kent in 1503, went to Eton and King's College, Cambridge, where he took his B.A. degree in 1525.[1] Besides a great love of learning, he 'had also a wonderful promptness of wit, and a ready capacity to receive and understand any thing, insomuch that he seemed not only to be sent unto learning, but also born for the same purpose. Neither was there any diligence wanting in him, equal unto that towardness, or worthy of his disposition; whereby it came to pass, that he was not only a lover of learning, but also became an exquisite learned man; in which exercise when he had diligently laboured certain years, not without great profit both of Latin and Greek, at last he fell into knowledge and acquaintance with William Tyndale, through whose instructions he first received into his heart the seed of the gospel and sincere godliness'.[2]

Tyndale, who had been Colet's favourite pupil at Oxford,[3] took his M.A. degree there in 1515, and then removed to Cambridge, where he resided probably from 1515 to 1521.[4] In 1523 and 1524 he was in London, and it was there that Frith assisted him in his translation of the New Testament into English. They may have met originally in Cambridge soon after Frith first came into residence.[5]

[1]D.N.B. Frith.   [2]J. Foxe, *Acts and Monuments*, Vol. 5 (1877 ed.), p. 4.
[3]T. M. Lindsay, *A History of the Reformation* (1934 ed.) Vol. 2, p. 319.
[4]D.N.B. Tyndale.
[5]D.N.B. Frith; M. L. Loane, *Masters of the English Reformation* (1954), pp. 54–56. *Cf.* M. L. Loane, *Pioneers of the Reformation in England* (1964), p. 4.

Archbishop Warham said in 1521 that Oxford was infected with Lutheranism,[1] so when Frith went there in 1525 he would soon find sympathetic companions. He was incorporated as a Junior Canon of Cardinal College (afterwards Christ Church), Wolsey's new foundation in that university, having been selected as one of the best scholars available to adorn that society.[2] He and his colleagues, a number of whom were like himself from Cambridge, were 'most picked young men, of grave judgment and sharp wits'; however, they, 'conferring together upon the abuses of religion, being at that time crept into the church, were therefore accused of heresy unto the cardinal, and cast into a prison', where several of them died.[3]

Frith and others were released in or soon after September, 1528,[4] on condition that they should not travel more than ten miles from Oxford. He, however, went abroad for a few years, during part of which he lived at the new University of Marburg, where he met many of the continental reformers; he again helped Tyndale, who had removed in 1524 to the Continent from England, in his literary work, and translated Patrick Hamilton's Latin theses of 1527 into English, having the book published as *Patrick's Places*.[5]

On his return home in 1532, Frith was apprehended and examined. He defended his beliefs so ably that Cranmer was greatly influenced in the same direction.[6]

---

[1]*Letters and Papers. Henry VIII*, Vol. iii, (1519–1523), p. 449. [2]*D.N.B.* Frith·
[3]Foxe, *op. cit.*, p. 5. *Cf. Letters and Papers. Henry VIII*, Vol. iv Part 2 (1526–1528), pp. 1158, 1762, 1804–1805, 2036; Part 3 (1529–1530), p. 2300. On the condition of the college, *cf.* also *ibid*. Vol. iv, Part 2, pp. 1220–1221, 1829, 2247.
[4]*Letters and Papers. Henry VIII*. Vol. iv, Part 2 (1526–1528), p. 2036.
[5]T. M. Lindsay, *A History of the Reformation* (1934 ed.), p. 280; M. L. Loane, *Pioneers of the Reformation in England* (1964), pp. 7–8: see further, W. A. Clebsch, *England's Earliest Protestants* (1964), pp. 78–85.
[6]A. Gray, *Cambridge University, An Episodical History* (1926), p. 133.

He was so successful in debating the concept of purgatory that he even converted one of his three opponents, Rastal, to his part.[1] Foxe notes that among Frith's other virtues, 'there was also in him a friendly and prudent moderation in uttering of the truth, joined with a learned godliness'.[2] Nevertheless, he was condemned for heresy and burnt at the stake in 1533 at Smithfield.[3]

[1]Compare the shock of Patrick Hamilton's defeat in discussion of Alexander Aless (Alesius), who at a later date became a firm Protestant, also the effect upon Bernard Gilpin of the arguments of Peter Martyr.
[2]Foxe, *op. cit.*, p. 9.   [3]*D.N.B.* Frith.

3

HUGH LATIMER c. 1490 ? – 1555

Conversion 1524

THE YEAR of Latimer's birth is not known; it has indeed been estimated within the remarkably wide range of no less than twenty-five years, between 1470[1] and 1494. This is due to sundry items of contemporary evidence, which are neither very clear nor entirely consistent. The difficulties are clearly set out by Demaus[2] and Chester.[3] However, his conversion certainly took place in 1524, when he says (in 1553) that he was 'thirty years of age'. If this figure be taken precisely and literally, he must have been born in 1493 or 1494; but he may have meant merely that he was then in his thirties, in which case his birth could be placed any time between 1485 and 1494, most likely about 1490.[4] He graduated B.A. and became a Fellow of Clare Hall, Cambridge, in 1510; M.A. 1514; B.D. 1524. He was ordained both Deacon and Priest in 1515.[5]

Ralph Morice, Archbishop Cranmer's secretary, wrote that Latimer, who, being noted for his holiness of life, had been made the keeper of the University Cross, was a zealous admirer of the school-doctors, such as Duns Scotus and Thomas Aquinas, that he perceived 'the youth of the university inclined to the reading of the scriptures, leaving off those tedious authors and kinds of study', that in the school of the

---

[1]So by W. Gilpin, *Life of Hugh Latimer* (1809) and E. L. Cutts, *Dictionary of the Church of England* (1895 ed.).
[2]R. Demaus, *Hugh Latimer* (1881).　　[3]A. G. Chester, *Hugh Latimer* (1954).
[4]*Cf.* Ed. G. E. Corrie, *Sermons of Hugh Latimer*, Parker Society (1844), pp. i–ii; H. C. Porter, *Reformation and Reaction in Tudor Cambridge* (1958), p. 44.
[5]*Alumni Cantabrigienses.*

university he 'most eloquently made to them an oration, dissuading them from this new-fangled kind of study, and vehemently persuaded them to the study of the school-authors', but that soon after doing so 'he was mercifully called to the contrary', for he was brought 'unto the knowledge of the truth of God's holy word by the godly lecture of divinity, read by Mr. George Stafford in the university school at Cambridge', so that this teaching 'of a Saul had, as it were, made him a very Paul'. This experience is described by G. E. Corrie as 'Latimer's First Conversion at Cambridge'.[1] Perhaps it was his initial awakening.

Stafford's lectures certainly had a great effect on Latimer, as also on many others of his auditors,[2] but the immediate cause of his actual conversion, as he records himself, was the action of Thomas Bilney. In the first of a course of seven sermons on the Lord's Prayer preached in 1552, Latimer stated:—'Bilney was the instrument whereby God called me to knowledge; for I may thank him, next to God, for that knowledge that I have in the word of God. For I was as obstinate a papist as any was in England, insomuch that when I should be made bachelor of divinity, my whole oration went against Philip Melanchthon and against his opinions. Bilney heard me at that time, and perceived that I was zealous without knowledge: and he came to me afterwards in my study, and desired me, for God's sake, to hear his confession. I did so; and, to say the truth, by his confession, I learned more than before in many years. So from that time forward I began to smell

[1]Ed. G. E. Corrie, *Sermons and Remains of Hugh Latimer*, Parker Society (1845), p. xxvii.
[2]H. C. Porter, *op. cit.*, p. 42; *cf.* J. Foxe, *Acts and Monuments*, Vol 4 (1877 ed.), p. 656.

the word of God, and forsook the school-doctors and such fooleries. Now, after I had been acquainted with him, I went with him to visit the prisoners in the tower at Cambridge; for he was ever visiting prisoners and sick folk. So we went together, and exhorted them as well as we were able to do; moving them to patience, and to acknowledge their faults'.[1]

In a sermon preached on Twelfth Day, 1553, Latimer said that 'all the papists think themselves to be saved by the law: and I myself have been of that dangerous, perilous, and damnable opinion, till I was thirty years of age. So long I had walked in darkness, and in the shadow of death!'[2]

Latimer again expressly acknowledged his debt to Bilney in his Conference with Ridley in prison in 1555:—'Sir, you make answer yourself so well, that I cannot better it. Sir, I begin now to smell what you mean: by travailing thus with me, you use me, as Bilney did once, when he converted me. Pretending as though he would be taught of me, he sought ways and means to teach me; and so do you. I thank you, therefore, most heartily'.[3]

As to the effects of Latimer's conversion, Foxe wrote:—'whereas before he was an enemy, and almost a persecutor of Christ, he was now an earnest seeker after him, changing his old manner of calumnying into a diligent kind of conferring, both with master Bilney and others, with whom he was often and greatly conversant.

After this his winning to Christ, he was not satisfied with his own conversion only, but like a true disciple of

[1]Sermons, op. cit. (1844), pp. 334–335.   [2]Sermons and Remains, op. cit (1845), p. 137.
[3]Ed. H. Christmas, The Works of Nicholas Ridley, Parker Society (1841), p. 118.

the blessed Samaritan, pitied the misery of others; and therefore he became both a public preacher, and also a private instructor to the rest of his brethren within the university, by the space of three years; spending his time partly in the Latin tongue amongst the learned, and partly amongst the simple people in his natural and vulgar language'.[1]

In spite of opposition, he and Bilney thus continued for a time in Cambridge, where they 'used much to confer and company together, insomuch that the place where they most used to walk in the fields, was called long after the heretics' hill'.[2]

It is only necessary to add that, as is very well known, he crowned his faithful witness by his martyrdom with Ridley in 1555.

---

[1] J. Foxe, op. cit., Vol. 7 (1877 ed.), p. 438.
[2] Ibid., p. 452. See also, M. L. Loane, Masters of the English Reformation (1954), pp. 10-13, 93-95.

4

PATRICK HAMILTON 1504 – 1528

Conversion 1526

PATRICK HAMILTON was the son of Sir Patrick Hamilton and Catherine Stewart, daughter of the Duke of Albany, who was a son of King James II of Scotland. The Abbey of Ferne was conferred upon him in 1517, so that he could more easily go abroad to study for the priesthood. He was educated at the University of Paris, where he became a Master of Arts in 1520 and where he was deeply influenced by the followers of Erasmus. After a sojourn at the University of Louvain he returned to Scotland, where he was incorporated as a member of the University of St. Andrew's in 1523.

In July, 1525, the Scottish Parliament enacted a law against importing Luther's works or propagating his opinions, and in the same year copies of Tyndale's New Testament were smuggled into Scottish ports. It is clear that Hamilton had meanwhile been carefully studying Lutheran teaching and comparing it with that of Erasmus, who desired a reform of discipline and organisation, but not of doctrine. During the course of the year 1526 Hamilton's own opinions had changed sufficiently to warrant the use of the word 'conversion', though as yet his conclusions were only tentative. He began then openly to declare his new convictions. In Lent, 1527, Archbishop James Beaton, inquiring into rumours on this subject, found that Hamilton was 'inflamed with heresy, disputing, holding and maintaining divers heresies of Martin Luther and his followers, repugnant to the faith',[1] and cited him to be summoned formally and accused.

11

Hamilton wisely fled to the Continent, where he was confirmed and established in the doctrines of the Reformation. He met Luther, Melanchthon and Bugen-hagen at Wittenberg; he witnessed the opening of the first Evangelical University at Marburg on May 30, 1527, where he was greatly influenced by the teaching of Franz Lambert and where also he lived for a time with William Tyndale. There too he composed some theses in Latin for the initial academic disputation. After some six months in Germany, he risked his life by returning to Scotland during the autumn of 1527 as a pioneer of reform, but after a heroic defence he met the inevitable doom of being burnt at the stake on February 29, 1528, at St. Andrew's.[2]

[1]P. Lorimer, *Patrick Hamilton* (1857), p. 82.
[2]T. M. Lindsay, *A History of the Reformation* (1934 ed.), p. 280; M. L. Loane, *Pioneers of the Reformation in England* (1964), pp. 7-8.

5

THOMAS FORRET ? – 1539

Conversion c.1530

'THOMAS FORRET, Vicar of Dollar was a gentleman of the house of the Laird of Forrets in Fife. His father was master stabler to King James IV. After he had gotten some beginning in the rudiments, he went to Cologne and learned his grammar, and by the help of a rich lady was sustained there at the schools. After he returned, he was made a Canon in Saint Colme's Inche (Inchcolm in the Firth of Forth), and was then a fervent Papist. There fell out a debate betwixt the abbot and the canons about their portion due to them for their maintenance. They got the book of their foundation, that they might understand the better what allowance was due to them every day.

The abbot took the book from them, and gave them a volume of Augustine's, to read and study instead of it. "O happy and blessed was that book!" said he many a time after, whereby he came to the knowledge of the truth. He converted the younger canons, "but the old bottles", he said, "would not receive the new wine". Thereafter, he was made Vicar of Dollar. He taught his flock the Ten Commandments, and shewed them the way of their salvation to be only by the blood of Jesus Christ. He penned a little catechism, which he caused a poor child answer him, when any faithful brother came to him, to allure the hearts of the hearers to embrace the truth, which indeed converted many in the country about.

He rose at six of the morning and studied till twelve,

and after dinner till supper in summer. In winter he burnt candle till bed time. When he visited any sick person in the parish that was poor, he would carry bread and cheese in his gown's sleeve to the sick person, and give him silver out of his purse, and feed his soul with the bread of life. He was very diligent in reading the Epistle to the Romans in the Latin tongue, whereby he might be able to dispute against the adversaries. He would get three chapters by heart in one day, and at evening gave the book to his servant, Andrew Kirk, to mark when he went wrong in the rehearsing; and then he held up his hands to the heavens, and thanked God that he was not idle that day.'[1]

He preached every Sunday on the Epistles and Gospels. His unusual industry and methods aroused suspicion, and he was summoned several times before the Bishop of Dunkeld; however, he succeeded in escaping further molestation until David Beaton became Archbishop of St. Andrew's in 1539; soon afterwards, he was apprehended, condemned, and burnt to death.[2]

---

[1]D. Calderwood, The History of the Kirk of Scotland, ed. T. Thomson, from the original MS. of c.1646, Vol 1 (1842), pp. 127–128. See further, ibid., pp. 124–127, 128–129.   [2]D.N.B. Forret.

6

DAVID STRAITON ? – 1534

Conversion 1534

'MR. CALDERWOOD from Knox, and both out of Fox, who had written attested accounts of this matter, gives the Laird of Dun's conversation, as the occasion of the conversion of David Straiton, a cadet of the house of Laureston, who was, with Norman Gourlay, a man of more learning, burnt for religion. It will not be an useless digression to give a hint of him here. Mr. Straiton was at first very ignorant, and hated the priests and Popish clergy only for their pride and avarice and from no principle. His business was much in fishing, and he had some vessels and servants employed in this way. The Bishop of Moray claimed the tithe of the fish. When the bishop's servants came to him in their Lord's name, to receive the tenth fish, he told them, if they would have what his servants had much toil in getting, he thought it was reasonable they should come and receive it where they (his servants) got the stock, and it was generally said that Mr. Straiton's servants had orders from him to cast every tenth fish they catched into the sea.

A process of cursing, as it was termed at that time, or the bishop's excommunication for non-payment of his tithes, was raised. This he contemned; and this year, 1534, he got a summons for heresy. A gracious God had mercy in store and work for him at his death, and at this time wrought a mighty change upon him. Mr. Straiton had been very stubborn, and even vicious; he despised all reading, especially in good purposes; but now he delighted in nothing but reading. He had been neglected in his education, and could not read himself; but after the Lord had awakened him, he was constantly pressing such as could to read to him; and he exhorted all to peace and love, and a contempt of the world, though he himself had been very quarrelsome and earthly minded. He frequented much the company of John Erskine, Laird of Dun, a man, say the three cited authors, marvellously enlightened for these times.

When the Laird of Laureston, a youth and nephew or some relation of his, was reading to Mr. Straiton on the New Testament and came to these words, "He that denieth me before men, him will I deny before my father which is in heaven and his angels", Mr. Straiton, now under summons, was extremely affected with them: they came in upon him with so much power, that he could not contain, but suddenly threw himself before all present on his knees, and extending his hands and looking constantly with his eyes toward heaven a reasonable time, he burst forth, at length, in these words: "O Lord, I have been wicked, and justly mayest thou abstract thy grace from me; but, O Lord, for thy mercy's sake, let me never deny thee, nor thy truth, for fear of bodily pain or death." This prayer of his was not poured out in vain, for a little after, in August, he was with the other condemned to be burnt, by the bishops, in the king's presence. After sentence, Mr. Straiton asked the king's grace. The bishops answered proudly, "The king's hands were bound, and he had no grace to give to such as by their law were condemned", and so they were both burned, August 27."[1]

[1] R. Wodrow (1679–1734), MS. *Collections upon the Lives of Reformers and Most Eminent Ministers of the Church of Scotland*—printed edition, Vol. 1 (1834), pp. 5–7.

7

JOHN HOOPER c. 1495 – 1555

Conversion c. 1540

JOHN HOOPER was born in Somerset, where his father was apparently a wealthy man. He took his B.A. degree at Oxford in 1519, 'after the study of the sciences, wherein he had abundantly profited'. He became a member of the Cistercian order at Gloucester, but when that monastery was dissolved in 1540 he went to live in London. There he became deeply impressed by some of the works of Zwingli and by Bullinger's Commentaries on St. Paul's Epistles. He read these most attentively and thoroughly, and then went back to Oxford to study the Bible, 'in the reading and searching whereof, as there lacked in him no diligence joined with earnest prayer; so neither wanted unto him the grace of the Holy Ghost to satisfy his desire, and to open unto him the light of true divinity.'

His efforts to propagate reformed teaching, however, speedily led him into difficulties, all the more so since the reactionary Six Articles of 1539 had not long before been enacted. He 'fell eftsoons into displeasure and hatred of certain rabbins in Oxford, who, by and by, began to stir coals against him; whereby, and especially by the procurement of Dr. (Richard) Smith (the Regius Professor of Divinity), he was compelled to void the University.'

A little later, he found it wiser to live abroad, and saw much of Bullinger at Zürich. In 1548 he returned to England, and in 1551 was consecrated Bishop of Gloucester. When Mary succeeded Edward VI, Hooper was soon imprisoned, and in 1555 he was burned to death at Gloucester.[1]

A few of the details recorded above rest on uncertain evidence and there are some alternative possibilities,[2] but it is quite certain that Hooper's conversion was occasioned by his reading Zwingli, Bullinger and the Scriptures, and that many years later he sealed his faith in martyrdom.

---

[1] J. Foxe, *Acts and Monuments*, Vol. 6 (1877 ed.), pp. 636–637; Ed. C. Nevinson, *Later Writings of Bishop Hooper*, Parker Society (1852), pp. vii–viii; D.N.B.
[2] *Cf.* C. H. E. Smyth, *Cranmer and the Reformation under Edward VI* (1926), pp. 95–96.

8

JOHN BRADFORD c. 1510 – 1555

Conversion 1547

JOHN BRADFORD was 'brought up in virtue and good learning from his very childhood'. He became proficient in Latin and arithmetic at school, while afterwards he was expert as an auditor and was paymaster of the army under Sir John Harrington. In 1547, he entered the Inner Temple to study law, but removed to Catharine Hall, Cambridge, the next year in order to prepare for Holy Orders. He already knew Latimer, and in 1549 Ridley, then Master of Pembroke Hall as well as Bishop of Rochester, invited him to become a fellow of Pembroke. He was a friend there of Bucer and the tutor of Whitgift. In 1550, he was ordained by Ridley, now Bishop of London, who appointed him one of his chaplains. In 1551, he was made a Prebendary of St. Paul's and one of the six chaplains of Edward VI. Shortly after the accession of Mary, Bradford was imprisoned, and in 1555 he was burned at the stake at Smithfield.

Bradford's conversion was described in 1574 by Thomas Sampson, his friend and probably the human agent of the complete transformation of his character. Sampson, who had studied in 1547 with Bradford in the Temple, wrote the Preface to *Two Sermons* made by Bradford, heading this Preface with the words:—'To the Christian Reader, Tho. Sampson wisheth the felicity of speedy and full conversion to the Lord,' and continuing:—' . . . I which did know him familiarly must needs give to God this praise for him, that among men I have scarcely known one like unto him. I did know when and partly how it pleased God, by effectual calling, to turn his heart unto the true knowledge and obedience of the most holy gospel of Christ our Saviour; of which God did give him such an heavenly hold and lively feeling, that, as he did then know that many sins were forgiven him, so surely he declared by deeds that he "loved much". For where he had both gifts and calling to have employed himself in civil and worldly affairs profitably; such was his love of Christ and zeal to the promoting of his glorious gospel, that he changed not only the course of his former life, as the woman did (Luke vii), but even his former study, as Paul did change his former profession and study. Touching the first, after that God touched his heart with that holy and effectual calling, he sold his chains, rings, brooches, and jewels of gold, which before he used to wear, and did bestow the price of this his former vanity in the necessary relief of Christ's poor members, which he could hear of or find lying sick or pining in poverty. Touching the second, he so declared his great zeal and love to promote the glory of the Lord Jesus, whose goodness and saving health he had tasted, that to do the same more pithily he changed his study . . .'

Bradford very soon proved the genuineness of his conversion by his conscientiousness over a matter of restitution, which involved him in the displeasure of his former employer, Sir John Harrington, and a considerable financial loss. He wrote confutations of Roman Catholic doctrines, meditations, prayers and sermons, and was noted for his exemplary life and piety.[1]

[1] The Writings of John Bradford—Sermons, Meditations, etc. (Parker Society) (1848), pp. 29–37; Letters, Treatises, etc. (1853), pp. xi–xliv.

9

BERNARD GILPIN 1517 – 1583

Conversion c.1563

BERNARD GILPIN entered the Queen's College, Oxford, at the age of sixteen, where he was much influenced by the writings of Erasmus and studied Scripture with close attention to Hebrew and Greek. He was elected a Fellow of his own College, but soon afterwards transferred to the new foundation of Christ Church. His conversion from Romanism was an extremely gradual one, based as it was on careful study, cautious reaction to events, and a natural dislike for argumentation. Yet there was a complete change in his religious opinions, the crisis of which appears to have come when he discovered, after the publication in 1563 of the decisions of the Council of Trent, that the Church of Rome 'had carried her authority to such an height of arrogance as to set up her own unwritten word against the Scriptures'.[1]

In 1575, he was persuaded to compose an account of what happened:—

'You require me to write, in a long discourse, the manner of my conversion from superstition to the light of the Gospel; which, I think you know, was not in a few years. As time and health will permit, I will hide nothing from you, confessing my own shame, and yet hoping with the apostle, "I have obtained mercy, because I did it ignorantly".

In King Edward's time I was brought to dispute against some assertions of Peter Martyr, although I have ever been given to eschew, so far as I might,

[1] W. Gilpin, *The Life of Bernard Gilpin* (1854), p. 13.

controversies and disputations. Being but a young student, and finding my groundwork not so sure as I supposed, I went first to the Bishop of Durham,[1] who told me that "Innocent the Third was much overseen, to make transubstantiation an article of faith". He found great fault with the Pope for indulgences, and other things.

After, I went to Dr. Redman, in whom I had great trust for the fame of his virtue and learning. He told me, "the communion-book was very godly, and agreeable to the Gospel". These things made me to muse.

Afterwards one of the Fellows of the Queen's College told me, he heard Dr. Chedsey say among his friends, "The Protestants must yield to us in granting the presence of Christ in the sacrament, and we must yield to them in the opinion of transubstantiation; so we shall accord".

Dr. Weston made a long sermon in defence of the communion in both kinds.

Mr. Morgan told me, that Mr. Ware, a man most famous both for life and learning, had told him before his death that the "chief sacrifice of the Church of God was the sacrifice of thanksgiving". This was his answer, when I desired to know what might be said for the sacrifice of the mass.

The best learned bishops, likewise, of this realm at that time withstood the supremacy of the Pope, both with words and writing.

Mr. Harding coming newly from Italy, in a long and notable sermon did so lively set forth, and paint in their colours, the friars, and unlearned bishops assembled at

[1]Cuthbert Tunstall, Bishop of London (1522-1530) and of Durham (1530-1559), who was Gilpin's uncle.

Trent in council, that he much diminished in me, and many others, the confidence we had in general councils.

All these things, and many more, gave me occasion to search both the Scriptures and ancient fathers, whereby I began to see many great abuses, and some enormities, used and maintained in popery, and to like well of sundry reformations on the other side.

Afterwards, in three years' space, I saw so much gross idolatry at Paris, Antwerp, and other places, that made me to dislike more and more the popish doctrines; especially because the learned men disallowed image-worship in their schools, and suffered it so grossly in their churches.

As I could with small knowledge, I examined the mass: the greatest fault I then found was too much reverence and gross worshipping of the gaping people, because I believed not transubstantiation. Likewise my conscience was grieved at the receiving of the priest alone. Yet at length I said mass a few times as closely as I could.

I reasoned with certain that were learned of my acquaintance, why there was no reformation of these great enormities about images, reliques, pilgrimages, buying mass and trentals, with many other things, which in King Edward's time the Catholics (so called) did not only grant to be far amiss, but also promised that the church should be reformed, if ever the authority came into their hands again. When I asked when this reformation was to begin, in hope whereof I was the more willing to return from Paris, I was answered, ''We may not grant to the ignorant people that any of these things hath been amiss: if we do, they will straight infer other things may be amiss as well as these, and go still further and further".. This grieved me, and made me seek for quietness in God's word: no where else I could find any stay.

After this, in two or three sermons at Newcastle, I began to utter my conscience more plainly, when thirteen or fourteen articles were drawn up against me and sent to the bishop. Here my adversaries of the clergy, whom I had sore offended by speaking against their pluralities, had that which they looked for. They caused the bishop to call me in their presence, and examine me touching the sacrament. The bishop showed favour so far, I trust, as he durst; urging me nothing with transubstantiation, but only with the real presence, which I granted, and so was delivered at that time. For the real presence, I was not then resolved, but took it to be a mystery above my capacity; yet my conscience was somewhat wounded for granting before them in plain words the thing whereof I stood in doubt.

After Queen Mary's death, I began to utter my mind more plainly. Before (I must needs confess my weakness) ignorance, and fear of enemies, had somewhat restrained me.

Thus, in process of time, I grew to be stronger and stronger; yet many grievous temptations and doubts have I had, which many nights have bereaved me of sleep.

My nature hath evermore fled controversy so much as I could. My delight and desire hath been to preach Christ, and our salvation by him, in simplicity and truth, and to comfort myself with the sweet promises of the Gospel, and in prayer'.[1]

[1]W. Gilpin, *op. cit.*, pp. 14–17. See further, G. Carleton, *The Life of Bernard Gilpin* (1629), pp. 32–41; J. Strype, *Annals of the Reformation* (ed. of 1824), Vol. 1, pp. 246–247.

Gilpin was Vicar of Norton in the Diocese of Durham from 1552 to 1553; then he travelled for three years to Mechlin, Antwerp, Ghent, Brussels, Louvain, and Paris, where he became more settled in his dislike of popery. Yet he risked returning to England during Queen Mary's reign and went at once to his uncle, who soon gave him the Archdeaconry of Durham and Rectory of Easington. He quickly met with opposition and found it advisable to resign these appointments. However, he then became Rector of Houghton, Queen Mary died, and all danger to his life was removed. His conversion from Romanism was in due time completed, but his attitude towards reformed teaching was very moderate and he did not approve the 'discipline' of the Puritans. He was greatly loved, was noted for his piety and diligence, and was called 'The Apostle of the North'. His charities were very extensive and included the founding of a grammar school, from which many scholars proceeded to the universities.[1]

[1]See further, D.N.B.

LAURENCE CHADERTON *c.* 1536 – 1640

Conversion *c.1565*

LAURENCE CHADERTON was born probably in 1536 or 1537 at Oldham, Lancashire, a son of Thomas Chaderton, 'a man of ancient family, of respectable position and good means, and a staunch upholder of the old faith'. In his youth he spent much time in hunting and hawking, but after leaving school he developed a great appetite for reading under a tutor, Laurence Vaux, a devoted Romanist, who successfully prepared him for the University of Cambridge.

'He entered at Christ's College (formerly God's House) in 1562', when he was already twenty-five or twenty-six years of age, 'and there studied with great assiduity; not, however, without shewing that the bodily vigours gained in his old pursuits might lead him into some scrapes. He joined with zeal in the quarrels which from time to time broke out between town and gown'.

'Whilst at Christ's he shared in the general feeling which was growing up in the country and university against the doctrines of the Roman Church. He seems to have gone through severe mental struggles on this subject. He deliberately examined the points in dispute between the *Reformati* and the adherents of the old faith; and with many and earnest prayers (*obnixe apud Deum assiduis precibus contendebat*) decided in favour of the Reformers. The result came, as such things do, from various sources – study of the Bible, the conversation of his fellows, and that mental agitation and movement which men look upon as "a call" from God.

His father by no means sympathised with his son's change of faith, and wished him to leave the University and proceed to the Inns of Court to study law, offering him an allowance of £30 a year (a liberal sum for the son of a simple esquire in those days) if he would do so. Laurence, by the advice of his friends, declined the offer, and thereupon received the following letter from his father:

"Dear Laurence,

If you will renounce the new sect which you have joined you may expect all the happiness which the care of an indulgent father can secure you; otherwise I enclose in this letter a shilling to buy a wallet with. Go and beg for your living. Farewell".[1]

It is fair to add that the angry parent relented a little, but only to the extent of a bequest in 1572 of £2 per annum for life.[2]

The son soon obtained a college scholarship, took his B.A. degree in 1567, and was elected a Fellow in 1568. Among his pupils was William Perkins. In 1584, Sir Walter Mildmay, who had been a fellow-commoner at Christ's and was a keen supporter of the reformed faith, founded Emmanuel College, and appointed Chaderton as its first Master. There he did a great work and remained till 1622, when he retired. He was also afternoon lecturer at St. Clement's Church for nearly fifty years, where his ministry converted many. He lived to an immense age, a most distinguished centenarian.[3]

[1]W. Dillingham, *Memoir of Laurence Choderton*, freely abbreviated and translated from the original Latin of 1700 by E. S. Shuckburgh (1884), pp. 2–4.
[2]*Ibid.*, p. 29.
[3]See further, J. Peile, *Biographical Register of Christ's College, Cambridge* (1910), Vol. 1, pp. 89–90; D.N.B.

ARTHUR HILDERSAM 1563 – 1631

Conversion c.1576

ARTHUR HILDERSAM, born on October 6, 1563, was the son of 'a gentleman of an ancient family'. 'He was brought up in the Popish manner, taught to say his prayers in Latin; both his parents and their kindred, especially his mother, being zealous Papists. When he was to be sent abroad to school, his father's aim was only to send him to a good school, where many gentlemen's sons were taught; but God so ordered it, (by his good providence) that his father unawares placed him at Saffron Walden School in Essex, with one Master Desborough, a godly man, and a religious Protestant, who, taking great affection to him for his wit and disposition, was very careful of him, and taught him not only that humane learning that was fitting for his years, but the grounds of the Protestant Religion. This his schoolmaster was the first blessed instrument that God was pleased to make use of to work in him a liking and relish of the Reformed Religion. He continued with him till he was fit for the University, which was not long. For when he was about thirteen years of age, he was placed by his father (the good hand of God still over-ruling him) with a very godly and religious tutor in Christ's College in Cambridge, where he continued till he was Master of Arts, where he gained much love and esteem for his piety, learning, ingenuity, affability, and harmless inoffensive witty converse'.[1]

---

[1]Ed. S. Clarke, *The Lives of Thirty-Two English Divines* ... (1677), pp. 114–115.

Meanwhile, about 1578, his father realised to his horror the change in his son's beliefs, tried unsuccessfully to persuade him to visit Rome, and cast him off; but fortunately a relative took charge of him and sent him back to his tutor at Cambridge. He took his M.A. degree in 1584, when he became a Fellow of Trinity Hall. He was for many years Vicar of Ashby-de-la-Zouch and was never a separatist, though he was often in difficulties for non-conformity.[1]

It is interesting to note that John Milton's father, who brought up his son as a Puritan, had himself been disinherited by his own parent, 'a zealous papist'.[2]

[1] *Alumni Cantabrigienses.*   [2] S. Johnson, *Lives of the English Poets* (1906 ed.),
Vol. 1, p. 64.

12

JOHN DOD 1555 – 1645

Conversion c.1582

JOHN DOD entered Jesus College, Cambridge, in 1572, became a Master of Arts there in 1579, and Fellow from 1578 to 1585.[1]

'The manner of his Conversion was thus. The Steward, or Boucher of the College, accused him to the Master, for the non-payment of a considerable sum of money due for one of his pupils, which Master Dod had truly paid, but he forgot to set it down. Hereupon there was a vehement contest betwixt them about this business, and the vexation of mind that he should be accounted a defrauder did so trouble Master Dod that he fell into a fever, and was dangerously sick; yet all this while he was but in a natural estate. For, though he had some good skill in the theoric part of Divinity, yet he was without any application; and his affliction was this, that he should be blamed for that, which he from the Law and light of nature hated. All his sorrow as yet was but worldly sorrow; and as himself says, he neither did nor could tell how to pray.

At length the Lord put into his heart that Scripture, *Romans* vii. 14, "The Law is spiritual, but I am carnal, and sold under sin", and presently his sins came upon him like armed men, and the tide of his thoughts was turned, and he left musing how he was wronged, and seriously considered how he had offended God, and he betook himself to great humiliation, and earnestly besought the Lord for pardon and peace in Jesus Christ. Yet for some time he could find no comfort, but going

[1] *Alumni Cantabrigienses.*

on to seek the Lord, there follows after much humiliation, much consolation, and the Lord sealed to him, that his sins were washed away with the blood of Christ. Then did he desire his accuser to come to him, and told him, that though he had accounted him to be his great enemy, yet now he acknowledged him to be his good friend, for that he was a means to bring him unto God. And afterwards it so fell out (by God's good Providence) that it came to this man's remembrance that Master Dod had paid him the money, and he was very sorrowful for the wrong which he had done him, and did him all the right he could for the healing of his name; and Master Dod said, that he had not a more faithful friend in all the College, during his abode there, than this man proved'.[1]

Dod was Rector of Hanwell, Oxfordshire, for twenty years, was then more than once suspended for nonconformity, but became Vicar of Fawsley, Northamptonshire, in 1624 and there remained for the rest of his very long life. Some of his writings were well known.[2]

[1]Ed. S. Clarke, *The Lives of Thirty-Two English Divines* . . . (1677), pp. 168–169.   [2]D.N.B.

13

WILLIAM PERKINS 1558 – 1602

Conversion c.1582

'WILLIAM PERKINS was born at Marton in Warwickshire in the year 1558 and educated in Christ's College, Cambridge. For some time after his going to the university, he continued exceedingly profane and ran to great lengths in prodigality. While Mr. Perkins was a young man and a scholar at Cambridge, he was much devoted to drunkenness. As he was walking in the skirts of the town, he heard a woman say to a child that was forward and peevish, "Hold your tongue, or I will give you to drunken Perkins, yonder". Finding himself become a by-word among the people, his conscience smote him, and he became so deeply impressed, that it was the first step towards his conversion . . .

When the Lord was pleased to convert him from the error of his ways, he immediately directed his attention to the study of divinity, and applied himself with such uncommon diligence, that in a short time he made incredible proficiency in divine knowledge'.[1]

Perkins matriculated at Christ's in 1577, took his B.A. degree in 1580 – 1 and was elected a Fellow in 1584. He was famous both for his numerous writings and for his preaching, especially at Great St. Andrew's Church, where he was Lecturer for many years and attracted many auditors both from the town and university.[2] He played a part in the conversion of numerous men, including, as we shall see, Blackerby,

---

[1] B. Brook, *The Lives of the Puritans*, Vol. 2 (1813), p. 129.
[2] J. Peile, *Biographical Register of Christ's College*, Vol. 1 (1910), pp. 141–142.

Cotton, Mather and Baxter.

In *A Grain of Mustard Seed* (1597), Perkins expounded his teaching on conversion:—'The conversion of a sinner is not wrought all at one instant, but in continuance of time, and that by certain measures and degrees. . . . (Yet) a sinner in the very first act of his conversion is justified, adopted, and incorporated into the mystical body of Christ'.[1]

[1] W. Perkins, *Works* (1616), Vol. 1, p. 637.

14

JOHN WELSH 1569 – 1622

Conversion c.1584

JOHN WELSH, a son of the Laird of Colliestoun in Nithsdale, was born in 1569. 'He was a rich example of grace and mercy, but the night went before the day, being a most hopeless extravagant boy. It was not enough to him frequently, when he was a young stripling, to run away from the school, and play the truant; but after he had passed his grammar, and was come to be a youth, he left the school and his father's house, and went and joined himself to the thieves on the English Border, who lived by robbing the two nations; and amongst them he stayed till he spent a suit of clothes. Then, when he was clothed only with rags, the prodigal's misery brought him to the prodigal's resolutions: so he resolved to return to his father's house, but durst not adventure till he should interpose a reconciler. So in his return homeward, he took Dumfries in his way, where he had an aunt, one Agnes Forsyth; and with her he diverted some days, earnestly entreating her to reconcile him to his father.

While he lurked in her house, his father came providentially to the house to salute his cousin, Mrs. Forsyth; and after they had talked a while, she asked him whether ever he had heard any news of his son, John: To her he replied with great grief, "O cruel woman, how can you name his name to me? The first news I expect to hear of him is that he is hanged for a thief". She answered, "Many a profligate boy had become a virtuous man", and comforted him. He insisted upon his sad complaint, but asked whether she knew his lost son was yet alive; she answered, Yes, he was, and she hoped he should prove a better man than he was a boy: and with that she called upon him to come to his father. He came weeping, and kneeled, beseeching his father for Christ's sake to pardon his misbehaviour, and deeply engaged to be a new man. His father reproached him and threatened him; yet at length, by the boy's tears and Mrs. Forsyth's importunities, he was persuaded to a reconciliation.

The boy entreated his father to put him to the college, and there to try his behaviour, and if ever thereafter he should break, he said he should be content his father should disclaim him for ever: so his father carried him home, and put him to the college, and there he became a diligent student of great expectation, and showed himself a sincere convert, and so he proceeded to the ministry',[1] having taken his M.A. degree at the University of Edinburgh in 1588.

'He gave himself wholly to ministerial exercises . . . But if his diligence was great, so it is doubted whether his sowing in painfulness or his harvest in success was greater: for if either his spiritual experiences in seeking the Lord, or his fruitfulness in converting souls, be considered, they will be found unparalleled in Scotland. And many years after Mr. Welsh's death, Mr. David Dickson, at that time a flourishing minister at Irvine, was frequently heard to say, when people talked to him of the success of his ministry, that the grape-gleanings in Ayr in Mr. Welsh's time were far above the vintage of Irvine in his own'.[2]

---

[1] J. Kirkton, The History of Mr. John Welsh, (1703), reprinted in Select Biographies, Ed. W. K. Tweedie, Vol. 1 (1845), pp. 1–2.
[2] Ibid., p.6.

15

RICHARD ROTHWELL *c.* 1563 – 1637

Conversion *c.1590*

RICHARD ROTHWELL's *Life* was written by Stanley
Gower of Dorchester; it was included among the biographies edited by Samuel Clarke. Rothwell 'had a
prompt wit, a quick apprehension, a clear understanding, a sound judgment, a ready speech, and a
strong memory . . . improved by diligent study. . . . He
was tall, well set, of great strength of body and activity,
of a stern countenance, of invincible courage, of
approved valour, and of a very goodly and majestic
presence'. He entered Queens' College, Cambridge, in
1578, took his B.A. degree in 1581, and was ordained
by Archbishop Whitgift of Canterbury. He preached
learnedly, but had no personal religious experience;
he abhorred 'debauchery and debauched companions,
. . . . but gave himself to hunting, bowling, shooting,
more than became a Minister of the Gospel, and sometimes he would swear'.

'He was playing at bowls amongst some Papists and
vain gentlemen upon a Saturday, somewhere about
Rochdale, in Lancashire; there comes into the green to
him one Master Midgley, a grave and godly Minister of
Rochdale, whose praise is great in the Gospel, though
far inferior to Master Rothwell in parts and learning;
he took him aside and fell into a large commendation
of him, at length told him what pity it was that such a
man as he should be a companion for Papists, and that
upon a Saturday when he should be preparing for the
Sabbath-day. Master Rothwell slighted his words and
checked him for his meddling.

The good old man left him, went home and prayed privately for him; Master Rothwell, when he was retired from that company, could not rest, Master Midgley's words struck so deep in his thoughts. The next day he went to Rochdale Church to hear Master Midgley, where it pleased God to bless that ordinance so, as Master Rothwell was by that sermon brought home to Christ. He came after sermon to Master Midgley, thanked him for his reproof, and besought his direction and prayers, for he was in a miserable condition of nature; and under the spirit of bondage he lay for a time, till afterwards, and by Master Midgley's hands also he received "the spirit of adoption", wherewith he was so sealed, that he never lost his assurance to his dying. Though he was a man subject to many temptations, the devil assaulting him very much, yet God was mightily with him, that out of his own experience he was able to comfort many. He esteemed and counted Master Midgley ever afterward for his spiritual father'. Rothwell became a Domestic Chaplain to the Earl of Devonshire and a Non-Conformist.[1]

---

[1]Ed. S. Clarke, *The Lives of Thirty-Two English Divines* . . . (1677), pp. 67–68; *Alumni Cantabrigienses.*

16

PAUL BAINES c. 1573 – 1617

Conversion c.1593

PAUL BAINES was admitted at Christ's College, Cambridge, in 1590 – 1, ' where his Conversation at first was so irregular, that his father being grieved at it, before his death, being intimately acquainted with one Master Wilson, a salesman in Birchin Lane, he left with him forty pounds by the year, desiring him, that if his son did forsake his evil course and become an honest man, he would then give him that forty pounds per annum, if not, that he would never let him have it.

But it pleased God, not long after his father's decease, to shew him his sins, and to work effectual repentance in him for the evil of his ways; so that, forsaking his former evil company and practices, he became eminent for piety and holiness, and according to that of our Saviour, "Much being forgiven him, he loved much". After which gracious change wrought in him by the goodness of God, it was not long before Master Wilson fell dangerously sick, and hearing how God had dealt with Master Baines, he sent for him, and desired him to pray with him, by which as also by his savoury discourse, finding that what he had heard of him rather came short of the truth than exceeded it, according to that trust reposed in him, perceiving himself to be upon his death-bed, he told Master Baines of the forty pounds per annum, which his father left with him, and so faithfully delivered up to him those writings of the agreement which had passed betwixt his father and him'.[1]

[1] Ed. S. Clarke, *The Lives of Thirty-Two English Divines* . . . (1677), p. 23.

Baines became a Fellow of his College in 1600, and lived a good, useful life, but perhaps his greatest importance lies in the fact that 'it pleased God to make him an instrument of the conversion of that holy and eminent servant of Jesus Christ, Doctor Sibbs'.[1]

---

[1]*Ibid.*, p. 25. *Cf. Ibid.*, pp. 143–145; And A. B. Grosart, *Memoir of Richard Sibbes* (1862), pp. xxxiv–xxxv. Details of this happening, which occurred probably about 1602–1603, have not been recorded.

17

RICHARD BLACKERBY 1574 – 1648

Conversion c. 1596

RICHARD BLACKERBY was born in 1574 at Worlington in Suffolk. His father gave to his ten children a
'pious education', and designed Richard, his second
son, 'from the first for the Ministry'[1]. He entered
Trinity College, Cambridge, at the age of fifteen, 'where
he lived nine years, and became an eminent scholar in
all parts of learning, especially in his great skill in the
Hebrew, Greek and Latin tongues . . .

While he was in the University, famous Mr. Perkins
was a preacher and lecturer in the Town of Cambridge,
upon whose ministry he diligently attended; whereby
his soul (when he was middle Bachelor of Arts) was
deeply wrought upon, and truly converted, but he lay
some years in great distress of conscience and much
perplexity of spirit, when his father took him for some
time home to Worlington, to see if change of air might
a little relieve him in his melancholy, which his friends
thought proceeded from temper of body, though it had
another cause, which neither air nor company could
remove.

After a short time, he desired to return again to Mr.
Perkins, for satisfaction of soul, and it pleased God (as
he was returning to Cambridge, and riding alone upon
Newmarket Heath, bemoaning his sad condition before
the Lord) to reveal his reconciled face in Christ Jesus
to him, and to give him that peace of conscience (so
well grounded, and so clearly evidenced) that he never

[1]Ed. S. Clarke, *The Lives of Sundry Eminent Persons* (1683), Part 1, pp. 57–58.

lost it to his dying day'. This moment of illumination completed his conversion, which had begun a few years earlier with his awakening by the preaching of Perkins.

In later life, Blackerby often delivered sermons in various churches, but he spent most of his time tutoring young men, including some who were preparing for the Ministry. He was noted for his great piety.[1]

[1]*Ibid.*, pp. 58–64.

18

ROBERT BOLTON 1572 – 1631

Conversion c.1603

ROBERT BOLTON was born in 1572, entered Lincoln College, Oxford, in 1592, but transferred to Brasenose, where he took his B.A. degree in 1596 and M.A. in 1602, became a Fellow the same year and College lecturer in logic, also in moral and natural philosophy.[1]

'But all this while (or for the most part), though he was very learned, yet he was not good . . . he loved stage-plays, cards and dice, he was a horrible swearer and Sabbath-breaker, and boon-companion'. He particularly disliked all who 'were of a strict and holy conversation' as being Puritans. However, at Brasenose, 'falling into the acquaintance of one Mr. Peacocke, Fellow of that House, a learned and godly man, it pleased God by his acquaintance to frame upon his soul that admirable workmanship of his repentance and conversion to eternal life'. The means of this transformation was violent, God 'laying before him the ugly visage of his sins which lay so heavy upon him, as he roared for grief of heart, and so affrighted him, as I have heard him say, he rose out of bed in the night for very anguish of spirit. And to augment his spiritual misery, he was exercised with foul temptations'. These 'continued for many months, but yet God gave him at length a blessed issue, and those grievous pangs in his spiritual birth produced two admirable effects in him . . . . an invincible courage and resolution for the cause of God, . . . secondly, a singular dexterity in comforting

[1]*Alumni Oxonienses; Dictionary of National Biography.*

afflicted and wounded spirits. . . . Upon this he resolved to enter into the Ministry, and about the thirty-first year of his age was ordained'.[1]

In his preaching, he 'aimed next to the glory of God at the conversion of souls, . . . many hundreds were either absolutely converted, or mightily confirmed, or singularly comforted in their grievous agonies by his ministry'.[2]

He took his B.D. degree in 1609, in which year he was instituted as Rector of Broughton, Northampton-shire, where he remained until his death in 1631.[3]

Cf. Samuel Clarke's account of the conversion of the Puritan Robert Bolton, upon whom the Lord acted with a vigor which He usually reserves for "such strong vessels, as he intendeth for strong encounters, and rare employ-ments; for the Lord ranne upon him as a Giant, taking him by the neck, and shaking him to pieces, as he did _Iob_; beating him to the ground as he did Paul, by laying before him the ugly visage of his sins, which lay so heavy upon him that he roared for anguish of heart" _The Marrow of Ecclesiastical History_, 2d ed. [1654], p. 925.

William H. Halewood, _The Poetry of Grace: Reformation Themes and Structures in English Seventeenth-Century Poetry_ (New Haven and London: Yale University Press, 1970), p. 63, n. 54.

[1] E. Bagshawe, _The Life and Death of Mr. Bolton_ (4th edition, 1639), pp. 11–17.
[2] _Ibid._, p. 19.   [3] _Alumni Oxonienses._

43

19

JOHN COTTON 1584 – 1652

Conversion c.1605

JOHN COTTON entered Trinity College, Cambridge, in 1598, where he was very industrious and successful; later he moved to Emmanuel College, 'that happy seminary, both of piety and learning: and in that Society the Lord gave him favour, so that in due time he was honoured with a Fellowship amongst them; when he was elected to it (in 1606) after a diligent and strict examination according to the Statutes of the College . . . He proved a diligent Tutor, and had many young Students committed to his care . . . His pupils were honourers and lovers of him: and he was a Tutor, a Friend, and a Father unto them.'

'The manner of his conversion, according to his own relation, was thus. During his residence in the University, God began to work upon him by the ministry of Master William Perkins of blessed memory: but the motions and strivings of his heart which then were he suppressed, thinking that if he should trouble himself with matters of religion, according to the light he had then received, it would be an hindrance to him in his studies, which then he had much addicted himself unto. Therefore he was willing to silence those suggestions and inward callings which he had from God's Spirit, and did wittingly defer the prosecution of that work until afterwards. At length, as he was walking in the fields, he heard the bell tolling for Master Perkins who lay a dying, whereupon he was secretly glad in his heart, that he should now be rid of him, who had (as he said) laid siege to and beleagured his heart. This became matter of much affliction to him afterwards, God keeping it upon his spirit, with the aggravation of it, and making it an effectual means of convincing him and humbling him in the sight and sense of the natural enmity that is in man's nature against God.

Afterwards, hearing Dr. Sibbes (then Mr. Sibbes) preaching a sermon about regeneration, wherein he showed, first, what regeneration was not, and so opening the state of a mere civil man, Master Cotton saw his own condition fully discovered, which (through God's mercy) did drive him to a stand, as plainly seeing himself destitute of true grace, all his false hopes and grounds now failing him: and so he lay for a long time, in an uncomfortable despairing way. And of all other things, this was his heaviest burden, that he had wittingly withstood the means and offers of grace and mercy which he found had been tendered to him. Thus he continued, till it pleased God to let in a word of faith into his heart, and to cause him to look unto Christ for his healing, which word also was dispensed unto him by the same Doctor Sibbes, which begat in him a singular and constant love to the said doctor, of whom he was also answerably beloved.'[1]

Cotton was ordained deacon and priest in 1610, was Vicar of Boston, Lincolnshire, 1612-1633, then went to New England and was Minister at Boston, Massachusetts, till his death in 1652.[2]

[1]Ed. S. Clarke, *The Lives of Thirty-Two English Divines* . . . (1677), pp. 217–218.
[2]*Alumni Cantabrigienses.*

20

JOHN PRESTON 1587 – 1628

Conversion c.1612

JOHN PRESTON entered King's College, Cambridge, in 1604, transferred to Queens' College, where he obtained a Fellowship in 1609, and from 1622 until his death was Master of Emmanuel College, where he succeeded Laurence Chaderton. Preston was ordained deacon and priest in 1614.[1]

John Cotton had a great reputation in Cambridge, so that, when he was about to deliver a University Sermon, 'the memory of his former accurate Exercises filled the colleges, especially the young students, with a fresh expectation of such elegancies of learning as made them flock to the sermon with an Athenian itch after some new thing, as to the ornaments of rhetoric and abstruser notions of philosophy. But his spirit now favouring of the cross of Christ more than of humane literature, and being taught of God to distinguish between the ''Word of Wisdom'' and the wisdom of words, ''his speech, and preaching, was not now with the enticing words of man's wisdom, but in the demonstration of the Spirit, and of power.''

The disappointed expectation of the auditory soon appeared in their countenances, and the discouragement of their non-acceptance returned him unto his chamber not without some sad thoughts of heart: where yet he had not been long, but lo, Doctor Preston (then Master Preston) knocks at his chamber door, and coming in, acquainted him with his spiritual condition, and tells him how it had pleased God to work effectually

[1]Alumni Cantabrigienses.

upon his heart by that sermon; after which Doctor Preston ever highly prized him, and both fully and strongly closed with him'.[1] Preston also soon became friendly with Dod and Hildersam, 'who would often come to his chamber'.[2] In 1624 Preston succeeded Sibbes' successor, Jeffries, as Lecturer at Holy Trinity Church, where he was followed by Goodwin in 1628.[3]

---

[1]Ed. S. Clarke, *The Lives of Thirty-Two English Divines* . . . (1677), pp. 218–219. *Cf. Ibid.*, pp. 78–79. See further, I. Morgan, *Prince Charles's Puritan Chaplain* (1957), pp. 18–20.　　[2]Clarke, *op. cit.*, p. 82.
[3]H. C. G. Moule, *Charles Simeon* (1892), pp. 32–33; H. C. Porter, *Reformation and Reaction in Tudor Cambridge* (1958), p. 262.

21

RICHARD MATHER 1596 – 1669

Conversion 1614

RICHARD MATHER was born in 1596 at Lowton, Lancashire, and was sent to school at Winwick, four miles from his home. While there he 'enjoyed the public ministry of one Mr. Palin, who was then preacher at Leagh, . . . by means whereof some illumination, though not a through conversion was wrought in him'. At the early age of fifteen he was chosen to be the master of a new school at Toxteth Park, near Liverpool. He was very successful in teaching his pupils and also had time to continue his own studies.

'The means of his conversion was partly by observing a strange difference between himself and sundry in that godly family of Mr. Edward Aspinwall, . . . a learned and religious gentleman; and Mr. Mather took notice of the way and walking of that holy man, which was such as himself had not yet been accustomed unto, which caused sad fears to arise in his soul, lest haply he might not be in the right way which leads unto eternal life'; he was also influenced by a sermon on John iii. 3 about 'the necessity of regeneration', preached by Mr. Harrison, 'a famous minister at Hyton'; and by reading a book written by William Perkins. 'God blessed these three things, not only to conviction, but to his conversion also; which was Anno Christi 1614.

The pangs of the new birth were very terrible to him, insomuch as many times when others were at their meals in the family where he sojourned, he often absented himself to retire under hedges and in other secret places, there to lament his misery before God. But after some time the Lord revived his broken heart, by sending the Holy Spirit to accompany the ministry of the Word, and to enable him to apply the precious promises of the Gospel to his soul'.[1]

He decided to go to the University of Oxford and was admitted to Brasenose College in 1618; but he stayed there only a few months, because the people of Toxteth entreated him to return to minister to themselves as well as to teach their children. The Bishop of Chester was sympathetic and soon ordained him. He was Minister at Toxteth and at Prescot, Lancashire, for fifteen years, was then suspended for nonconformity, and in 1635 he removed to New England, where he remained until his death in 1669.[2]

[1]Ed. S. Clarke, *The Lives of Sundry Eminent Persons* (1683), Part 1, pp. 126–128.
[2]*Alumni Oxonienses*; *Dictionary of National Biography*.

22

SAMUEL WINTER 1603 – 1666

Conversion c.1615

SAMUEL WINTER was born at Balsal, Warwickshire, in 1603 'of religious parents'. When he 'was about twelve years old, it pleased God, by the ministry of one Mr. Slader, then preacher at the Chapel of Knowl, in Balsal parish (if I mistake not) who, in a special manner was brought thither by Samuel's father's interest, and industry, to awaken his conscience, and to make him serious about the things which concerned his everlasting salvation; as also to stir up in him earnest desires of doing good to the souls of others; for which end one day as he came from school, about a mile from his father's house, he retired himself under a hedge to pray; and among other petitions, he begged of God that he would qualify and fit him for the work of the ministry, and make his labours effectual and successful therein: at which time he (at least thought that he) heard a voice saying to him; ''God hath heard thy prayer, and designed thee for that work, and thou shalt be an instrument of converting many souls to God.'' This exceedingly cheered up his heart, insomuch as, coming home, he applied himself to his father, humbly requesting that he might be trained up for the ministry. His father asked him the reason of those desires. He told him, what a prayer he had made to God, and what return he had from God to it. His father, being much affected therewith, soon after sent him to the Free School in Coventry' and later to Cambridge.[1]

[1]Ed. S. Clarke, *The Lives of Sundry Eminent Persons* (1683), Part 1, p. 95.

He took his B.A. degree at Emmanuel College, Cambridge, and in after life was best known as Provost of Trinity College, Dublin, from 1652 to 1660, where was a D.D. He died in 1666.[1]

---

[1]*Alumni Cantabrigienses*; *Dictionary of National Biography.*

23

ALEXANDER HENDERSON 1583 – 1646

Conversion 1615 – 1616

ALEXANDER HENDERSON was born in 1583 in Fife; he matriculated at St. Salvator's College, St. Andrew's, in 1599, took his M.A. degree in 1603, and became a Professor in the Faculty of Arts in 1610. 'At this period, Henderson was a strong advocate for Episcopacy, and in favour with the men in power.' Archbishop Gladstanes about 1613 presented him to the benefice of Leuchars, but the people were fervently Presbyterian and disapproved of the appointment.

On the day appointed for his induction, 'means had been previously taken to secure the church doors on the inside, so that no entrance could be effected by them. In spite of public opinion thus so strongly manifested, Henderson and his friends got into the church by a window, and went quietly through the solemnities of the occasion. For a time he was held, in the estimation of his flock, as a hireling and a stranger. Whatever might be his other merits, an interest in the spiritual welfare of his flock was not then of the number. Slightly impressed with the sacredness of his new calling, he was mainly anxious to support the principles in which he had been educated. But ere he had been more than two or three years in his parish, a change began insensibly to be wrought in his mind'.

Gradually 'a generous anxiety to be useful in guiding his people to godliness' took increasing hold of him. Then one day he went to hear a famous champion of the Presbyterian cause, Robert Bruce of Kinnaird, preach not far away on the words: "He that entereth not by the door into the sheepfold, but climbeth up some other way, the same is a thief and a robber"—St. John x. 1. Henderson 'felt at once as if the opinions he had hitherto entertained were founded in quicksand. The text, and sermon which followed it, sent home to his conscience, and accompanied by the blessing of God' was 'the turning point of his life'. It occurred in 1615 or 1616.[1]

'After this wonderful change on his sentiments, which went much deeper than a conversion to Presbyterianism, Henderson continued to discharge the duties of his retired parish in a manner much more conducive to the edification of his people', while 'ever after he retained a great affection for Mr. Bruce, whom he called his spiritual father'.[2]

He lived an eventful life as a leading Presbyterian minister and died in 1646.[3]

[1]J. Aiton, The Life and Times of Alexander Henderson (1836), pp. 86–95.
[2]T. McCrie, Sketches of Scottish Church History (1843), p. 225.
[3]Cf. Dictionary of National Biography.

24

THOMAS GOODWIN 1600 – 1680

Conversion 1620

THOMAS GOODWIN, who was born in 1600, was brought up in a Puritan environment and, as he says himself, 'I began to have some slighter workings of the Spirit of God from the time I was six years old'. He matriculated at Christ's College, Cambridge, in 1614. There he was greatly impressed with the holiness of life of several of its members and was often deeply pious himself, studying religious writings and attending Sibbes' preaching; but he became anxious to gain academic applause and to look for advancement. In this he succeeded, for, transferring to Catharine Hall in 1620, he took his M.A. and was elected a Fellow there that same year. Meanwhile, his devotional life was getting a little thin and he was sometimes neglectful of prayer.

At such a time, he records, 'when I was thus given over to the strength of my lusts, and further off from all goodness than ever I had been, and utterly out of hope that God would ever be so good unto me as to convert me', he was persuaded by a friend, on hearing a bell toll for a funeral, to attend the service. 'I was never so loath to hear a sermon in my life. Inquiring who preached, they told me it was Dr. Bambridge (Thomas Bainbrigge, a Fellow of Christ's College), which made me the more willing to stay, because he was a witty man. He preached a sermon which I had heard once before. . . . He spoke of deferring repentance, and of the danger of doing so. Then he said that every man had his day; it was "this thy day", not

to-morrow, but to-day. . . . The matter of the sermon was vehemently urged upon the hearer. . . . I was so far affected, as I uttered this speech to a companion of mine that came to church with me, and indeed that brought me to that sermon, that I hoped to be the better for this sermon as long as I lived. . . . This was on Monday the 2nd of October, 1620, in the afternoon'·
He had intended to spend some time with friends at Christ's, but he returned instead quietly to Catharine Hall.

'I thought myself to be as one struck down by a mighty power. The grosser sins of my conversation came in upon me, which I wondered at, as being unseasonable at first; and so the working began, but was prosecuted still more and more, higher and higher: and I endeavouring not to think the least thought of my sins, was passively held under the remembrance of them, and affected, so as I was rather passive all the while in it than active, and my thought held under, whilst that work went on. . . .

I knew no more of that work of conversion than these two general heads, that a man was troubled in conscience for his sins, and afterwards was comforted by the favour of God manifested to him. And it became one evidence of the truth of the work of grace upon me, when I reviewed it, that I had been so strangely guided in the dark. In all this intercourse, and those that follow to the very end, I was acted all along by the Spirit of God being upon me, and my thought passively held fixed. . . . An abundant discovery was made unto me of my inward lusts and concupiscence, . . . at which I was amazed, to see with what greediness

¹T. Goodwin, *Works* (1861 edition), Vol. 2, pp. lii–lv.

I had sought the satisfaction of every lust'.[1]

'I observed of this work of God upon my soul, that there was nothing of constraint or force in it, but I was carried on with the most ready and willing mind, and what I did was what I chose to do. With the greatest freedom I parted with my sins, formerly as dear to me as the apple of my eye, yea, as my life, and resolved never to return to them more. . . . I considered what I was doing, and reckoned with myself what it would cost me to make the great alteration. . . .

But the most eminent property of my conversion to God, I have been speaking of, was this, that the glory of the great God was set up in my heart as the square and rule of each and every particular practice'.[1]

Goodwin, who took his B.D. degree in 1630, exercised a notable ministry at Holy Trinity Church, Cambridge, from 1628 to 1634 as Lecturer and from 1632 to 1634 also as Vicar, after which he ministered in London and in Holland, having for conscientious reasons become an Independent. Seven years after his departure from Cambridge, on returning to England, he says, 'I had for some years after, well-nigh every month, serious and hearty acknowledgment from several young men, who had received the light of their conversion by my ministry while I was in the University of Cambridge'.[2] He was a member of the Westminster Assembly and chaplain to Oliver Cromwell. He served also as President of Magdalen College, Oxford, from 1649 to 1660 and took his D.D. degree at Oxford in 1653. He died in 1680.[3]

[1]*Ibid.*, pp. lxv–lxvi. [2]*Ibid.*, p. lxvi.
[3]J. Peile, *Biographical Register of Christ's College*, Vol 1 (1910), pp. 295–296; A. G. Matthews, *Calamy Revised* (1934), p. 228; H. C. G. Moule, *Charles Simeon* (1892), pp. 33–34; H. C. Porter, *Reformation and Reaction in Tudor Cambridge* (1958), pp. 272–273; *Dictionary of National Biography*.

25

SIR MATTHEW HALE 1609 – 1676

Conversion c.1630

WITH a view to his being ordained, Matthew Hale, who was born in 1609, was sent to some schools under Puritan influence and to Magdalen Hall, Oxford, where he matriculated in 1626. 'But the stage-players coming thither, he was so much corrupted by seeing many plays, that he almost wholly forsook his studies. By this he not only lost much time, but found that his head came to be thereby filled with such vain images of things that they were at best improfitable, if not hurtful to him; and being afterwards sensible of the mischief of this, he resolved upon his coming to London (where he knew the opportunities of such sights would be more frequent and inviting) never to see a play again, to which he constantly adhered'.

He was compelled to leave the university after three years of residence without taking a degree in order to be present at the defence of part of his estate in a law suit in London. There he 'set himself to many of the vanities incident to youth; but still preserved his purity, and a great probity of mind. He loved fine clothes, and delighted much in company'. He became an expert fencer, and thought of becoming a soldier, but decided instead on the law, entering Lincoln's Inn on November 8, 1629, 'being then deeply sensible how much time he had lost, and that idle and vain things had over-run and almost corrupted his mind'. He studied with great assiduity, and 'threw aside all his fine clothes'.

'Yet he did not at first break off from keeping too much company with some vain people, till a sad accident drove him from it, for he with some other young students, being invited to be merry out of town, one of the company called for so much wine, that notwithstanding all that Mr. Hale could do to prevent it, he went on in his excess till he fell down as dead before them, so that all that were present were not a little affrighted at it, who did what they could to bring him to himself again. This did particularly affect Mr. Hale, who thereupon went into another room, and shutting the door, fell on his knees, and prayed earnestly to God, both for his friend, that he might be restored to life again, and that himself might be forgiven for giving such countenance to so much excess; and he vowed to God, that he would never again keep company in that manner, nor drink a health while he lived: his friend recovered, and he most religiously observed his vow, till his dying day. . . .

This wrought an entire change on him: now he forsook all vain company, and divided himself between the duties of religion, and the studies of his profession'.[1] He became a most eminent lawyer, composed a number of works both on law and theology, and was noted for his wisdom and piety. He was elected M.P. for the University of Oxford in 1658–1659, was appointed Lord Chief Baron of the Exchequer in 1660, knighted in 1661, and created Chief Justice of the King's Bench in 1671. He died in 1676.[2]

---

[1] G. Burnet, *The Life and Death of Sir Matthew Hale* (1682), pp. 4–10.
[2] *Dictionary of National Biography*; *Alumni Oxonienses*. Cf. also, J. H. Overton, *Life in the English Church*, 1660–1714, (1885), pp. 116–117.

26

RICHARD BAXTER 1615 – 1691

Conversion c.1630

RICHARD BAXTER was born in 1615 at a village in Shropshire. His father was a freeholder; neither poor nor wealthy. The clergy and readers in the district were not learned or devout, as he notes in his autobiography:—'But though we had no better teachers, it pleased God to instruct and change my father, by the bare reading of the Scriptures in private, without either preaching or godly company, or any other books but the Bible: and God made him the instrument of my first convictions, and approbation of a holy life, as well as of my restraint from the grosser sort of lives. When I was very young, his serious speeches of God and the Life to Come possessed me with a fear of sinning. . . . At first my father set me to read the historical part of the Scripture, which suiting with my nature greatly delighted me; and though all that time I neither understood nor relished much the doctrinal part and mystery of redemption, yet it did me good by acquainting me with the matters of fact, and drawing me on to love the Bible, and to search by degrees into the rest'.

He was displeased that his father was maliciously called 'Puritan, Precision and Hypocrite', and he 'was fully convinced that godly people were the best, and those that despised them and lived in sin and pleasure were a malignant unhappy sort of people: and this kept me out of their company, except now and then when the love of sports and play enticed me.'

When he was a pupil at the Free School at Worcester, 'it pleased God of his wonderful mercy to open my eyes with a clearer insight into the concerns and case of my own soul, and to touch my heart with a livelier feeling of things spiritual than ever I had found before: and it was by the means and in the order following; stirring up my conscience more against me, by robbing an orchard or two with rude boys, than it was before; and being under some more conviction for my sin, a poor day-labourer in the town . . . had an old torn book which he lent my father, which was called *Bunny's Resolution* (being written by Parsons the Jesuit, and corrected by Edmund Bunny).[1] I had before heard some sermons and read a good book or two, which made me more love and honour godliness in the general; but I had never felt any other change by them on my heart. Whether it were that till now I came not to that maturity of nature, which made me capable of discerning; or whether it were that this was God's appointed time, or both together, I had no lively sight and sense of what I read till now. And in the reading of this book (when I was about fifteen years of age) it pleased God to awaken my soul, and shew me the folly of sinning, and the misery of the wicked, and the unexpressible weight of things eternal, and the necessity of resolving on a holy life, more than I was ever acquainted with before. The same things which I knew before came now in another manner, with light, and sense and seriousness to my heart.

This cast me first into some fears of my condition; and those drove me to sorrow and confession and prayer, and to some resolution for another kind of life; and many a day I went with a throbbing conscience,

[1] *A Book of Christian Exercise, appertaining to Resolution* . . . (1584). *Cf. D.N.B.* Bunny.

and saw that I had other matters to mind, and another work to do in the world, than ever I had minded well before.

Yet whether sincere conversion began *now*, or *before*, or *after*, I was never able to this day to know; for I had before some love to the things and people which were good, and a restraint from other sins except those forementioned; and so much from those that I seldom committed most of them, and when I did, it was with great reluctancy. And both now and formerly I knew that Christ was the only mediator by whom we must have pardon, justification, and life; but even at that time, I had little lively sense of the love of God in Christ to the world or me, nor of any special need of him. . . .

And about that time it pleased God that a poor pedlar came to the door that had ballads and some good books: and my father bought of him Dr. Sibbes' *Bruised Reed.*[1] This also I read, and found it suited to my state, and seasonably sent me; which opened more the love of God to me, and gave me a livelier apprehension of the mystery of redemption, and how much I was beholden to Jesus Christ.

All this while neither my father nor I had any acquaintance or familiarity with any that had any understanding in matters of religion. . . .

After this we had a servant that had a little piece of Mr. Perkins' *Works* (of *Repentance*, and the right *Art of Living and Dying well*, and *the Government of the Tongue*); and the reading of that did further inform me, and confirm me. And thus (without any means but

[1] Both his *Bruised Reed* (1630) and *The Soul's Conflict* (1635) exercised a wide influence.

books) was God pleased to resolve me for himself.'[1]

William Orme, in his introduction to Baxter's *Works*, considered that Baxter was the pioneer in writing in English about conversion. He had been induced to undertake this work by Archbishop Usher. Needing to awaken his uneducated and irreligious hearers at Kidderminster, Baxter wrote:—1. *Treatise of Conversion, preached and now published for the use of those that are strangers to a true conversion, especially the grossly ignorant and ungodly* (1657); 2. *A Call to the Unconverted to turn and live, from the Living God* (1657); 3. *Directions and Persuasions to a Sound Conversion* . . . (1658); 4. *Now or Never* (1663); and 5. *Directions to the Converted* . . . (1669). Of these, the second was famous and was translated into many languages. It resulted in the conversion of great numbers of people. The tone was one of deep earnestness and affection; it did not mince matters, but was kindly and sympathetic.[2]

[1] R. Baxter, *Reliquiae Baxterianae*, published from his original manuscript, written in 1664, by M. Sylvester (1696), pp. 1–4.
[2] R. Baxter, *Works*, Vol. 1 (1830), pp. 485–500.

27

GEORGE FOX 1624 – 1690-91

Conversion 1647

THE parents of George Fox were godly people and their son from early childhood was notably grave and serious. He was deeply religious, had an acutely tender conscience and was highly critical of those whose conduct did not appear to him to correspond with their profession. He had a mystical temperament, was subject to frequent dreams, visions and voices, and believed himself to be the recipient of direct divine revelation. In 1643 he left his home, wandered about the country, earnestly seeking satisfaction for his soul. At times he was almost in despair and was generally miserable, but sometimes he had 'great openings of the Scriptures'. He consulted various people whom he met, but they could not greatly help him – 'my troubles continued, and I was often under great temptations; I fasted much, and walked abroad in solitary places many days, and often took my Bible, and went and sat in hollow trees and lonesome places till night came on; and frequently, in the night, walked mournfully about by myself: for I was a man of sorrows in the times of the first workings of the Lord in me. . . . Though my exercises and troubles were very great, yet were they not so continual but that I had some intermissions, and was sometimes brought into such a heavenly joy, that I thought I had been in Abraham's bosom.'

By the year 1647 he had given up consulting all ministers of religion; 'for I saw there was none among them all that could speak to my condition. And when all my hopes in them and in all men were gone, so that I had nothing outwardly to help me, nor could I tell what to do; then, oh! then I heard a voice which said, "There is one, even Christ Jesus, that can speak to thy condition": and when I heard it, my heart did leap for joy. Then the Lord did let me see why there was none upon the earth that could speak to my conditiont namely, that I might give Him all the glory; for all are concluded under sin, and shut up in unbelief, as I had been, that Jesus Christ might have the pre-eminence, who enlightens, and gives grace and faith and power. Thus when God doth work, who shall let it? and this I knew experimentally. My desires after the Lord grew stronger, and zeal in the pure knowledge of God, and of Christ alone, without the help of any man, book, or writing. For though I read the Scriptures that spake of Christ and God, yet I knew Him not, but by revelation, as He who hath the key did open, and as the Father of Life drew me to His Son by His Spirit. Then the Lord gently led me along, and let me see His love, which was endless and eternal, surpassing all the knowledge that men have in the natural state, or can get by history or books; and that love let me see myself, as I was without Him.'

This was the crisis of the religious experience of George Fox, a veritable conversion, and it led him during that same year, 1647, to believe that God had called him to preach the gospel. 'The Lord opened my mouth, and the everlasting truth was declared amongst them, and the power of the Lord was over them all. For in that day the Lord's power began to spring, and I had great openings in the Scriptures. Several were convinced in those parts, and were turned from dark-

ness to light, and from the power of Satan unto God;
and many were raised up to praise God.'[1]

[1]*Journal of George Fox* (1694), Chapter 1. Everyman's Library Edition (1924), pp.7–11.

28

MARY, COUNTESS OF WARWICK
1624 – 1678

Conversion 1649

MARY BOYLE was a daughter of Richard Boyle, who became the first Earl of Cork. She married Charles Rich, fourth Earl of Warwick. Her life was written by her pastor and friend, Dr. Anthony Walker, shortly after her death.

'As to her beginning to be seriously religious, and to make it her business in good earnest. Though she had a good education, and had been principled in the grounds of catechism in her youth, yet she would confess she understood nothing of the life and power of religion upon her heart, and had no spiritual sense of it, till some years after she was married. She hath told me also with what prejudice and strange apprehensions, as to matters of religion, she came into the family in which she lived and died with so much honour, for she was almost frighted with the disadvantageous account which was given of it. But when she came to see the regular performance of Divine worship, and to hear the useful, edifying, preaching of the most necessary, practical, and substantial truths, and observed the order and good government, and received encouragement from her right honourable father-in-law, who had always an extraordinary value for and affection to her, her prejudice wore off, and approbation followed.

God made use of two more remote means of her conversion – afflictions and retirement. The Divine wisdom and grace is very adorable for adapting suitable means to bring his purposes to pass – as these were in her circumstances; for she would since acknowledge, that her great difficulty and hindrance were her love of the pleasures and vanities of the world, which she neither knew how to reconcile with the strictness of religion nor yet could be content to part with, for that whose sweets and better pleasures she was not then acquainted with. God therefore gradually weaned her by rendering more insipid what had too much pleased her, and by giving her vacancy and freedom from distraction to acquaint herself more thoroughly with the things of God. By which she was enabled to set her seal to that testimony which God gives to spiritual wisdom, that "her ways are ways of pleasantness, and all her paths are peace". And to her friends she would frequently and freely do it; assuring them that she had no cause to repent the change she had found, of the solid and satisfying pleasures she obtained, in religion, for those unquiet, empty ones she left in the ways of vanity: thereby encouraging them to try, not doubting but upon experience they would become of the same mind.

Two more immediate helps which God blessed to her were – the preaching of the word, which God hath ordained for the salvation of them that believe, 1 Cor. i. 21; and Christian conference; and (because such a hint may do others good) the pressing the necessity of speedy and true repentance, and showing the danger of procrastination, and putting off, and stifling present convictions by delay. This seemed to turn the wavering, trembling balance, and to fix the scale of her resolution.

This is about nine and twenty years since (i.e., 1649,

twenty-nine years since 1678), from which time (though before her conversation was viceless, sweet, and inoffensive, yet she would confess her mind was vain) she walked with God most closely, circumspectly, accurately.'[1]

Her *Diary* was published in part and attained great popularity. She was noted for her hospitality and charity.[2]

[1]A. Walker, *Memoir of Lady Warwick* (c. 1884 edition), pp. 23–25; *Cf.* Ed. S. Clarke, *The Lives of Sundry Eminent Persons* (1683), Part 2, pp. 168–169 (taken from Walker's *Memoir*).
[2]J. H. Overton, *Life in the English Church*, 1660–1714 (1885), pp. 142–144.

29

JOHN GIFFORD ? – 1656

Conversion c.1650

JOHN GIFFORD 'was born in the county of Kent; after-wards he became a major in the King's army during the civil wars. He was concerned in the insurrection raised (in 1648) in that county; for which he was apprehended, and, together with eleven others, received the sentence of death. But, the night before he was to suffer, his sister coming to visit him, and finding the sentinels who kept the door of the prison fast asleep, and his com-panions in a state of intoxication, she urged him to embrace the favourable opportunity and escape for his life. Having made his escape, he fled into the fields and crept into a ditch, where he remained about three days, till search for him was over; and then, by the help of friends, he went in disguise to London.

After concealing himself for some time in the city, and at various places in the country, he went to Bedford, where, though an entire stranger, he com-menced the practice of physic; but still remained very debauched in his life. He was greatly addicted to drunkenness, swearing, gaming, and similar immoral practices. In his gaming he usually found himself a loser, which made him sometimes discontented, and resolve to leave off the practice; but his resolutions were soon broken, and he returned to his old course. One night, having lost fifteen pounds, he became almost outrageous, attended with most reproachful thoughts of God; but looking into one of Mr. Bolton's books, something laid fast hold upon his conscience, and brought him for the first time to a deep sense of his sins. Under these painful convictions he laboured for about a month, when God by his word so discovered to him the forgiveness of his sins, through faith in Jesus Christ, that, as he used to say, he never lost sight of it afterwards.

Mr. Gifford, having thus tasted that the Lord was gracious, presently sought an intimate acquaintance with the religious people in Bedford, whom he had before grievously persecuted, and had even resolved to murder the minister who had occasionally preached to them. Indeed, he had been a man of so profligate and base a character, that they were for some time jealous of his profession; but he, being naturally of a bold spirit, still thrust himself among them, both in their public meetings and private company. Having made sufficient trial, they embraced him as a disciple and a brother; and after some time he began to preach among them. The very first sermon he preached was made instrumental in the conversion of a female, whose future life became an ornament to her profession.

He afterwards collected the most pious persons in the congregation together; and, having repeatedly assembled and prayed to God for his direction and blessing, they formed themselves into a Christian church. They were twelve in all, including Mr. Gifford, and all ancient and grave Christians, and well known to one another.' They unanimously chose Mr. Gifford as their pastor, and he accepted the charge from that time, about 1650, until his death in 1656.[1]

---

[1]B. Brook, *The Lives of the Puritans* (1813), Vol 3, pp. 257–259; taken from Meen's MS. *Collection*, pp. 313–317, 325; as transcribed from the original *Church-Book* at Bedford.

30

JOHN JANEWAY 1633 – 1657

Conversion c.1651

JOHN JANEWAY, whose life-story was told by his younger brother, James, was one of a large family of delicate children, born to religious parents. He made exceptional progress in Latin, Greek, Hebrew and Mathematics at a very early age, and went to Eton as a foundation scholar and King's College, Cambridge, of which he became a Fellow in 1654.

Meanwhile, when he was about eighteen years old, he was converted 'by the exemplary life, and heavenly and powerful discourse of a young man in the college, whose heart God had inflamed with a love to this precious soul, whereupon he took the first opportunity to set upon this hopeful plant, and God's Spirit did so set home wholesome instructions and counsel, with such evidence and power, that they proved effectual for his awakening out of his spiritual lethargy. The rather, being accompanied with the profitable and powerful preaching of those two able and worthy Divines, Dr. Arrowsmith and Dr. Hill, together with his reading several parts of Mr. Baxter's *Everlasting Rest*.[1]

Now a strange alteration might easily be discerned in the man: He now looked quite another way to what he had done formerly. . . . Now Mr. Janeway began to cast about how he might best improve what he did already know, and to turn all his studies into the right channel: Grace did not take him off from, but made

[1]First published in 1650.

him more diligent and spiritual in his studies: And now Christ was at the end and bottom of every thing.'[1]

[1]James Janeway, *Invisibles, Realities, Demonstrated in the Holy Life and Trium-phant Death of John Janeway* (1885 edition), pp. 13–19. (The first edition was published in 1673). Cf. also, Ed. S. Clarke, *The Lives of Sundry Eminent Persons* (1683), Part 1, pp. 60–62.

31

JOHN BUNYAN 1628 – 1688

Conversion c.1654

JOHN BUNYAN was born at Elstow, near Bedford, in 1628. He tells the story of his spiritual development in his famous autobiography, *Grace Abounding*, which was first published in 1666. From the outset, he emphasises God's mercy to him:—'the Lord did work his gracious work of conversion upon my soul.'

As a child, he says that he was noted for profanity, yet even then he trembled at thoughts of the day of judgment and was terrified by dreams and visions. As a young man, he records that he was the ringleader of his associates 'into all manner of vice and ungodliness'. He was alienated from religion.

However, about 1648 he married a young woman, whose father, 'a godly man', had bequeathed to her at his death *The Plain Man's Path-Way to Heaven*, by Arthur Dent, and *The Practice of Piety*, by Lewis Bayly, Bishop of Bangor, 1616–1632. On reading these books with her, he soon became a very devout and regular church-goer. One of the sermons of the village parson about the evil of breaking the sabbath day greatly impressed him, and he became deeply convicted of sin that same day while in the midst of a game:—' a voice did suddenly dart from Heaven into my soul, which said, "Wilt thou leave thy sins and go to Heaven? or have thy sins, and go to Hell?" At this I was put to an exceeding maze.' He came to the conclusion that it was too late for him to repent, and 'went on in sin with great greediness of mind.' About a month later, he was reproved by a woman for swearing, and told that he was setting a very bad example to all the youth of the neighbourhood.

He promptly gave up his cursing habits, took pleasure in reading the historical parts of the Bible, 'fell to some outward reformation, both in my words and life, and did set the Commandments before me for my way to Heaven.' He fancied that God must now be very pleased with him; the local people regarded him as a reformed character. After about a year he left off bell-ringing and gave up dancing as unsuitable for a religious man.

But one day he heard a few poor women in Bedford talking 'about a new birth, the work of God on their hearts, also how they were convinced of their miserable state by nature: they talked how God had visited their souls with his love in the Lord Jesus, and with what words and promises they had been refreshed, comforted, and supported against the temptations of the Devil.' This led him at once to long for the same happy experience; he sought 'the company of these poor people' and 'began to look at the Bible with new eyes', especially studying St. Paul's Epistles; he also met John Gifford, the pastor of the independent church which had been formed in Bedford in 1650.

Although Bunyan eagerly desired assurance of salvation, he was afraid that he might be a cast-away, and he was tempted to despair. Texts from scripture alternately depress and cheer him; his mind oscillates between fear and hope; he is helped by a copy of Luther's *Commentary on Galatians*; but he is tortured continually 'for the space of a year' by mental suggestions 'to sell and part with Christ'; he resists strongly, but then adds:—
'I felt the thought pass through my heart, "Let him go

if he will!" and I thought also that I felt my heart freely consent thereto.' This betrayal could only lead to 'the Judgment to come; nothing now for two years together would abide with me, but damnation, and an expectation of damnation . . . save some few moments for relief.' He suspects that he may have committed the unforgiveable sin against the Holy Ghost.

Towards the end of this period of his acute distress and violent spiritual struggles, passages from scripture of a more reassuring character gradually came to predominate in his mind:—'these words did with great power break in upon me, "My grace is sufficient for thee", . . . three times together'; and, some time later, 'This scripture also did now most sweetly visit my soul, "And him that cometh to me I will in no wise cast out", *John* vi. 37.' He now closely examines those verses in the Bible which had alarmed him and concludes that they were not applicable to him; still he remains uncertain.

'But one day, as I was passing in the field, and that too with some dashes on my conscience, fearing lest yet all was not right, suddenly this sentence fell upon my soul, *Thy righteousness is in Heaven*; and methought withal, I saw with the eyes of my soul Jesus Christ at God's right hand, there, I say, as my righteousness; so that wherever I was, or whatever I was a doing, God could not say of me, *He wants my righteousness*, for that was just before him. I also saw moreover, that it was not my good frame of heart that made my righteousness better, nor yet my bad frame that made my righteousness worse: for my righteousness was Jesus Christ himself, *the same yesterday, and to-day, and for ever, Heb.* xiii .8.

Now did my chains fall off my legs indeed, I was

loosed from my affliction and irons, my temptations also fled away: so that from that time those dreadful scriptures of God left off to trouble me; now went I also home rejoicing, for the grace and love of God: So when I came home, I looked to see if I could find that sentence, *Thy righteousness is in Heaven*, but could not find such a saying, wherefore my heart began to sink again, only that was brought to my remembrance, *He of God is made unto us wisdom, righteousness, sanctification, and redemption*; by this word I saw the other sentence true, *I Cor. i. 30.*'

'Further, The Lord did also lead me into the mystery of union with this Son of God, that I was joined to him, that I was flesh of his flesh, and bone of his bone, and now was that a sweet word to me in *Ephes. v. 30.* By this also was my faith in him, as my righteousness, the more confirmed to me; for if he and I were one, then his righteousness was mine, his merits mine, his victory also mine.' This was the turning-point in his long drawn out conversion experience, but it was not the end of all his temptations to doubt, which lasted a little longer.

All that needs to be added here is that Bunyan became a full member of the separatist congregation in Bedford about 1655 and that he became a preacher in 1656. He was imprisoned in 1660 for many years because he would not promise not to preach again. But it is for his writings that he is famous, not least for *Grace Abounding*.

32

JAMES FRASER 1639 -- 1699

Conversion c.1657

JAMES FRASER wrote his own autobiography. He describes 'four steps' in 'God's dealing with me while under some common work of the Spirit, and not fully converted' up to the age of seventeen. The first two steps comprised 'the zealous performance of some duties, especially prayer.' The third step, occasioned, when he was fifteen years old, by reading *The Practice of Piety*, led him to make 'conscience of all duties; and therefore meditated, read the Scriptures frequently, and kept the Sabbath very strictly, and reading of good books. And I left off all my old sins and ways, such as lying, swearing, and made conscience of all moral virtues; I left my gaming, my idle talk, and became very temperate . . . and yet a stranger to Christ, and lying fast bound in a natural condition . . . I had the very characters of a formal Pharisee.' In the fourth step, he was convinced of 'the vanity of formality in duties' by reading a book called *The Seventeen False Rests* and the words in *The Confession of Faith*: "That though one should form his life never so exactly, according to nature and morality, without Christ he could not be saved." This led to a period of almost three years of uncertainty, 'wherein I was settled in nothing but in a waiting and seeking condition.'

'Being at the University (of Edinburgh), and being at the age of seventeen or eighteen years, our minister proposed to celebrate the Sacrament of the Lord's Supper, of which he gave warning the Sabbath preceding the celebration thereof, I purposed (I know not upon what ground) to partake thereof . . . I knew I was in an unconverted condition, and that, if betwixt that day and the next Lord's Day, I were not converted, I would draw on myself a very grievous evil; and that, eating unworthily, I might give over hopes of ever thereafter being converted. . . . I went to sermon, and I found a better relish in the sermon than I had wont to find, and had an ear to hearken more attentively than at other times. After we were gone from church, I spent the rest of the day in spiritual exercises, and so was continuing very diligent in seeking the Lord, growing daily in the knowledge and love of his ways, seeing a beauty, and finding a relish that I never knew before.'

But by the Wednesday evening he had suffered a reaction; he was discouraged and doubted if he should communicate; however, he 'resolved to set the next day apart for fasting, and therein to seek God, hoping that these extraordinary means might do something. Hanging, therefore, by this small thread, I went to prayer with many sad complaints; and the Lord, while I was like the prodigal son a great way off, ran to meet me. I addressed myself to speak to the Lord Christ, and then was there a Gospel view given me of him; and some considerations and representations of Christ were brought into my mind, that he was the Mediator, a friend and Saviour to poor sinners, their only helper, the way, and the truth, and the life, that died for them, and one willing to be reconciled . . .

While I was thus exercised, a marvellous light shined on my understanding, and with the eyes of my mind, not of my body, I saw that Just One in his glory, and love, and offices, and beauty of his person; such a sight as I never did see anything like it, and which did so swallow me up as I turned speechless, and only said, "What is this? And where am I now?" The glory, love, and loveliness of Jesus, revealed to me, did very far exceed all that ever I saw or could see in the world, insomuch that there was no comparison. I was drawn by this, and after I had recovered, I said, "O Lord, thou hast overcome me! Heart and hand, and all that I have, is thine; I am content to live and die with thee." . . .

There followed upon this such liberty as I thought I could spend the whole night in prayer. Now was I persuaded that I was converted, and was come to that pitch which formerly I wanted; and all the clouds vanished which were betwixt the Lord and my soul. . . . . Nor did I think that my happiness could be equalled by any; and now was I fully content to communicate.'[1]

---

[1]Ed. W. K. Tweedie, *Select Biographies*, Vol. 2 (1847)—*Memoirs of the Rev. James Fraser of Brae . . .*, written by himself, pp. 89–112; *Cf.* A. Whyte, *James Fraser, Laird of Brae* (1911), pp. 24–39.

33

SARAH HOWLEY c. 1655 – 1670

Conversion c.1664

JAMES JANEWAY (younger brother of John), who was
born about the end of 1636 and died in 1674, published
in 1671 the first part and in 1672 the second part of
*A Token for Children, being an Exact Account of the
Conversion, Holy and Exemplary Lives and Joyful Deaths
of several Young Children.* Sarah Howley was the first
of the thirteen examples which he records. This book
attained great popularity and was often reprinted.

'Sarah Howley, when she was between eight and
nine years old, was carried by her friends to hear a
sermon, where the minister preached upon Matthew
xi. 30, "My yoke is easy, and my burden is light": in
the applying of which scripture, this child was mightily
awakened, and made deeply sensible of the condition
of her soul, and her need of Christ; she wept bitterly
to think what a case she was in; and went home and got
by herself into a chamber, and upon her knees she
wept and cried to the Lord as well as she could, which
might easily be perceived by her eyes and countenance.

She was not contented at this, but she got her little
brother[1] and sister into a chamber with her, and told
them of their condition by nature, and wept over them,
and prayed with them and for them.

After this she heard another sermon upon Proverbs
xxix. 1, "He that being often reproved hardeneth his
neck, shall suddenly be destroyed, and that without
remedy": at which she was more affected than before,

---

[1]Was he an ancestor of William Howley (1766–1848), Archbishop of Canterbury (1828–1848)?

and was so exceeding solicitous about her soul that she spent a great part of the night in weeping and praying, and could scarce take any rest day or night for some time together, desiring with all her soul to escape from everlasting flames, and to get an interest in the Lord Jesus; O what should she do for Christ! what should she do to be saved?

She gave herself much to attending upon the word preached, and still continued very tender under it, greatly favouring what she heard.

She was very much in secret prayer, as might easily be perceived by those who listened at the chamber door, and was usually very importunate, full of tears.

She would scarce speak of sin, or be spoken to, but her heart was ready to melt.

She spent much time in reading the scripture, and a book called *The Best Friend in the Worst of Times*; by which the work of God was much promoted upon her soul, and was much directed by it how to get acquaintance with God, especially toward the end of that book. Another book that she was much delighted with, was Mr. Swinnock's *Christian Man's Calling*, and by this she was taught in this measure to make religion her business. *The Spiritual Bee*[1] was a great companion of hers.

She was exceeding dutiful to her parents, very loath to grieve them in the least; and if she had at any time (which was very rare) offended them she would weep bitterly.

She abhorred lying, and allowed herself in no known sin.

[1] *The Spiritual Bee; or a Miscellany of Divine Meditations*, by an university pen, Oxford (1662)—probably by Nicholas Horsman or William Penn.

She was very conscientious in spending of time, and hated idleness, and spent her whole time either in praying, reading, instructing at her needle, at which she was very ingenious.

When she was at school, she was eminent for her diligence, teachableness, meekness, and modesty, speaking little; but when she did speak, it was usually spiritual.'[1]

She had a serious illness when about fourteen years of age, and died in the full assurance of God's love on February 19, 1670.

'Op. cit. (ed. of 1763), pp. 1–3.

34

THOMAS TREGOSSE *c.* 1634 – 1670

Conversion 1665

THOMAS TREGOSSE was born at St. Ives in Cornwall.
His parents were godly Puritans and gave their son a
pious education. He matriculated at Exeter College,
Oxford, in 1652 and took his B.A. in 1655, then
returned to St. Ives, where 'the inhabitants invited him
to be their minister,' and he was 'set apart for the work
of the ministry' on August 17, 1657. He moved thence
in October, 1659, to the Vicarage of Mylor and Mabe,
but was silenced by the Act of Uniformity of August
24, 1662. In September, 1663, he departed to the
parish of Budock, and there 'kept up his Lord's-day
meetings, many flocking to him.'

In January, 1665, 'his old sins were livelily presented
to him. Hereupon he betook himself to his duties, but
drove on very heavily. . . . Sometimes in reading, the
Lord would set home threatening, then comforting
Scriptures to keep him equally balanced between hopes,
that he might not sink, and fears, that he might not
presume. He was detained for about five weeks'
space under much bondage and afflictive terrors, with
little or no discoveries of God's gracious disposition;
till about the beginning of February, being under a
resolution to reveal some sins which burdened his
conscience, he met with a passage in an English Divine,
touching the greatness and freeness of Christ's love and
purchase; which, the Lord setting home, he was a little
quieted and refreshed by. The next day being the
Lord's-day, he had a sweet heart-melting consideration
of his sins, together with a lively contemplation of

Christ pierced; to whom he directed an eye of faith. . . .

And from this time he dated his conversion; for, albeit his conversation for some considerable time before was irreproachable, and his labours in the work of the ministry indefatigable; yea, and his zeal for Non-conformity remarkable; yet he judged the whole of his foregoing life, zeal, and labour in the ministry, to be no other than a continued series of formality and hypocrisy; . . . and withal he bewailed the Church of England, in that generally men were made ministers before they were made Christians.' It was noted also 'that, though he was before this time a constant and faithful preacher, yet he could not say the Lord had given him any convert as the fruit of his ministry, though he received many seals thereof afterward.'[1]

---

[1] T. Gale, *The Life and Death of Thomas Tregosse* (1671), pp. 2-11; *Cf.* Ed. S. Clarke, *The Lives of Sundry Eminent Persons* (1683), Part 1, pp. 109-112; *Alumni Oxonienses.*

35

SIR ALAN BRODERICK 1623 – 1680

Conversion c.1675

ALAN BRODERICK matriculated at Magdalen Hall, Oxford, in 1639, was created M.A. in 1661, was called to the bar at Gray's Inn in 1648, became a knight in 1660, and served as Member of Parliament for Oxford from 1660 to 1679, also as Surveyor-General in Ireland.[1]

Nathaniel Resbury, Vicar of Wandsworth, Surrey, preached at Broderick's funeral a sermon, which was printed in 1681. In this, he said:—'I will readily acknowledge (and why indeed should I scruple to own what himself with such repeated contrition and brokenness of spirit would to all sober ears so freely and heartily condemn himself for?) that a long scene of his life had been acted off in the sports and follies of sin: if I may use his own words, it was a pagan and abandoned way he had sometime pursued,[2] scepticism itself not excepted, wherein the poignancy of his wit, and the strength of his reasoning . . . may have been the occasion of a great deal of mischief towards some that are already gone to their accounts without the happy retreat that himself made; and others who may yet survive him, and ought to improve the goodly example he hath given them, of rescuing themselves from those ruinous illusions, wherein their misopiniated wit, and deceitful charms of their own lusts have hampered and entangled them.

But I mention these things, and I hope all good minds will entertain them with that kind of joy, which the

[1]*Alumni Oxonienses.*
[2]*Cf. Diary of Samuel Pepys*, under dates November 28, 1665, and December 19, 1666.

angels themselves are said to express at the conversion of a sinner, Luke xv. 7, 10. A joy (if I may so speak) that had been wanting in heaven, had it not been for the recovery of some profligate wanderers on earth; a pleasure which the indulgent father could not have conceived, had not the prodigal son returned to himself and him.'

As regards church order, 'his profession was that of the Reformed, as the doctine and discipline of it is established in the Church of England by law.' As regards 'his practice: This for some years last past (to which myself have been an eye-witness, and a joyful observer) hath been so signally religious, that . . . herein (how late soever he set out) yet when he once began the course, he made such large and nimble steps heaven-ward, that he out-stripped the ordinary passenger that had begun long before in self-denial and the zeal of his devotions, in circumspection and watchfulness over his actions and thoughts, in largeness of mind both for and toward God, in all the exercises of a deep and serious repentance, and in all the noble reasonings of faith beyond what is observable in the common stages of Christianity.'[1]

[1]N. Resbury, *Funeral Sermon on Sir Alan Broderick* (1681), pp. 11–14.

36

JOHN I. WILMOT,

SECOND EARL OF ROCHESTER 1647 – 1680

Conversion 1680

JOHN WILMOT, 'poet and libertine', succeeded his father, the first Earl of Rochester, on his death in 1657-8. He entered as a fellow-commoner in 1659-60 at Wadham College, Oxford, was created M.A. in 1661, travelled abroad, and in 1664 became a courtier at Whitehall, where he was soon attached to 'the most dissolute set'. He indulged in many notorious exploits, and in 1679 his 'health failed'. Much to his friends' astonishment, he read that autumn while convalescing the first volume, just published, of *The History of the Reformation*, by Gilbert Burnet. 'He invited the author to visit him, and encouraged him to talk of religion and morality.' The following spring, he listened with attention to the words of his chaplain, Robert Parsons, and then on June 25 wrote to Burnet, who came to him on July 20 and stayed till July 24, the earl dying two days later.[1]

That same year a book appeared, entitled: *Some Passages of the Life and Death of the Right Honourable John, Earl of Rochester . . . Written by his own Direction on his Death-Bed*, by Gilbert Burnet. The author says that his frequent visits between October, 1679, and April, 1680, included 'a long and free conversation with him for some months',[2] and that 'the three chief things we talked about were morality, natural religion,

[1]*Dictionary of National Biography. Cf.* also, *Alumni Oxonienses*; and J. Tillotson, *Works* (1752), Vol. 1, pp. xx–xxi.

[2]*Op. cit.*, p. 30.

and revealed religion, Christianity in particular.'[1] The details of these discussions are recorded at length,[2] the issue of which was:—'He told me, he saw vice and impiety were as contrary to humane society, as wild beasts let loose would be; and therefore he firmly resolved to change the whole method of his life: to become strictly just and true, to be chaste and temperate, to forbear swearing and irreligious discourse, to worship and pray to his Maker: and that though he was not arrived at a full persuasion of Christianity, he would never employ his wit more to run it down, or to corrupt others.'[3]

The earl's letter, dated June 25, 1680, says: 'Bestow your prayers upon me, that God would spare me (if it be his good will) to show a true repentance and amendment of life for the time to come: or else if the Lord pleaseth to put an end to my worldly being now, that He would mercifully accept of my death-bed repentance.'[4] Burnet gives details of his last visit,[5] when the Earl told him that 'he was now persuaded both of the truth of Christianity, and of the power of inward grace.'[6] In particular, he had been so moved when his chaplain read Isaiah liii to him, 'that he did ever after as firmly believe in his Saviour, as if he had seen him in the clouds.'[7] Further, the earl said: 'He was sure his mind was entirely turned, and though horror had given his first awakening, yet that was now grown up into a settled faith and conversion.'[8]

Writing at a later date, Burnet maintained his opinion at the time that the conversion was complete:– 'I do verily believe he was then so entirely changed,

[1] *Ibid.*, p. 35. [2] *Ibid.*, pp. 35–125. [3] *Ibid.*, p. 125. [4] *Ibid.*, p. 134.
[5] *Ibid.*, pp. 138–157. [6] *Ibid.*, p. 140. [7] *Ibid.*, pp. 141–142. [8] *Ibid.*, p. 148.

that if he had recovered he would have made good all his resolutions.'[1]

Robert Parsons, in *A Sermon preached at the Funeral of John, Earl of Rochester* (1680), says, in his Dedication to the earl's mother and widow, that they could both 'largely attest the truth of most of the remarkable occurrences that I have taken notice of during his Lordship's penitential sickness', and had desired the publication of the sermon. He also appeals[2] as witnesses to the reality of the conversion 'to all sorts of persons who in considerable numbers visited and attended him, and most particularly to those eminent physicians who were near him.' Moreover, he observes:[3] God has 'at last graciously heard the prayers of his nearest relations, and true friends, for his conversion and repentance; and 'tis the good tidings of that especially, what God has done for his soul, that I am now to *publish and tell abroad to the world*, not only by the obligations of mine office, in which I had the honour to be a weak minister to it, but by his own express and dying commands.'

The story of the earl's conversion, which created a great sensation at the time, was also told that same year in *The Libertine Overthrown* and in a broadsheet entitled, *The Two Noble Converts*, the other one being James Ley, third Earl of Marlborough (1618–1665), who was converted about 1664.[4]

Samuel Johnson, in his *Lives of the English Poets*, says of Rochester that 'with an avowed contempt of all decency and order, a total disregard to every moral, and a resolute denial of every religious obligation, he

---

[1]*History of My Own Time* (ed. of 1897), Vol. 1, p. 477. (Published posthumously, 1st ed. 1723).
[2]*Op. cit.*, pp. 33–34. [3]*Ibid.*, pp. 1–2. [4]*Dictionary of National Biography.*

lived worthless and useless, and blazed out his youth and his health in lavish voluptuousness', but that during his illness 'he received such conviction of the reasonableness of moral duty, and the truth of Christianity, as produced a total change both of his manners and opinions.'[1]

[1]*Op. cit.* (ed. of 1906), Vol. 1, pp. 155–156. (1st ed. 1779).

PSYCHOLOGY AND THE
CONVERSION EXPERIENCE

1   Pre-Conversion

THE SPIRITUAL BACKGROUND

THE FIRST eleven stories, from Thomas Bilney to Arthur Hildersam, are all of conversion from Rome; so far as evidence is available, they were probably brought up in homes and schools where religious faith and practice obtained; but this very likelihood made a change of allegiance difficult and when it occurred could be expected to result in family opposition, as clearly did happen in the cases of Chaderton and Hildersam. Parental anxiety for their offspring is evident in the lives of John Welsh and Paul Baines, both of whom rebelled against their authority in youth. Richard Blackerby was given a pious education and designed for the ministry from the outset. Samuel Winter's parents were devout and sympathetic. Thomas Goodwin was brought up in a Puritan environment, as also were Matthew Hale, George Fox and Thomas Tregosse. John Janeway was a child of religious parents. The outstanding example of a father's influence upon his son's spiritual development appears to be that of Richard Baxter's father, who had himself been instructed and changed by the private reading of the Bible.

THE MENTAL BACKGROUND

BILNEY, Latimer, Bradford, Chaderton, Hildersam, Dod, Perkins, Baines, Cotton, Preston, Goodwin and Janeway were all Fellows of Colleges at Cambridge,

Chaderton and Preston being also the first two Masters of Emmanuel College, while Goodwin was President of Magdalen College, Oxford. Frith, after graduating at King's College, Cambridge, was selected by Wolsey as one of the best scholars of his time to be a Junior Canon of Cardinal College, Oxford. Gilpin and Bolton were Fellows of Colleges at Oxford. Rothwell, Blackerby and Winter were Cambridge graduates, the last-named becoming afterwards Provost of Trinity College, Dublin. Hooper, Tregosse, Broderick and Wilmot were Oxford graduates. Hamilton graduated at Paris, Welsh at Edinburgh, and Henderson at St. Andrew's, where he was later a Professor. Hale and Baxter were men of outstanding ability.

GENERAL ENVIRONMENT

THE AGE of the Reformation, being one of religious questioning, excitement and upheaval, was thereby favourable to change of opinion and to spiritual discovery. The new learning had led to openness of mind and the translation of the Scriptures into the vernacular to deep religious experiences. But conversions from medieval doctrine resulted in many martyrdoms in England and Scotland, until the road to reform was cleared. Bilney, Frith, Latimer, Hamilton, Forret, Straiton, Hooper and Bradford were all burned to death for their faith between 1528 and 1555. Gilpin, Chaderton and Hildersam may be said to have moved in complete sincerity with the times in which they lived – a perfectly natural development, the spirit of the age assisting conversions not achieved without difficulties. Puritan theology, with its emphasis on original sin and individual salvation, was wholly favourable to the experience of religious conversion; so too was the serious attitude taken to life. Many of those whose stories are here related were earnest seekers after truth and needed a crisis to bring them to certainty. Some had lived disreputable lives, so that their conversions were more spectacular; such were Perkins, Welsh, Baines, Bolton, Gifford, Broderick and, most notably, Wilmot.

THE PERIOD OF AWAKENING

(Factors leading to awakening, acute dissatisfaction and divided personality)

THE FIRST eight subjects of this study were brought up as Romanists and with the exception of Straiton were all keen participants in religious observances. But, living when they did, and being of studious dispositions, they were exposed to new ideas. The effects of the debate between medieval and reformed tenets is even more clearly seen in the lives of Gilpin, Chaderton and Hildersam, all of whom likewise left the Roman fold. Awakening for them was a long, gradual process, leading first to uncertainty of belief and mental struggle.

The succeeding narratives are of a different character. Dod was exasperated by a false accusation of dishonesty, but this natural anger led to a spiritual awakening as soon as he began to consider 'how he had offended God'; Welsh followed his own inclinations until they brought him to want; Rothwell's self-esteem was shaken by a reproof; Blackerby was awakened by the preaching of Perkins; Bolton's change began through his friendship with Peacocke; the awakening of Cotton was caused by the sermons of Perkins, whose teaching he resisted, and of Sibbes; while one of Cotton's sermons initiated Preston's conversion; Mather was illuminated to some extent at school by the preaching of Palin; Henderson was disturbed by the hostility of his parishioners and he began to be anxious about their spiritual welfare; Goodwin had some religious experience from his childhood, and as an undergraduate was pious and helped by Sibbes' sermons, but then came a period of decline; Hale was distressed at the amount of time which he had lost in pursuing unprofitable impulses; Baxter was attracted by his father's example and teaching and his own study of the Bible; Fox was serious, devout and mystical from early life; Mary, Countess of Warwick, was alarmed at her introduction to the family into which she had married; Bunyan's wedding and the reading of devotional manuals with his wife made him very zealous for a time; Fraser prayed earnestly, read the Bible and *The Practice of Piety* and other good books, kept the Sabbath strictly and was acutely conscientious; the awakening of Wilmot was caused by his illness and fear of imminent death.

THE RESULTS OF AWAKENING

(The period of storm and stress)

BILNEY SPEAKS of the guilt of his sins and of 'being almost in despair', having tried fasting and other observances without avail; Gilpin refers to 'many grievous temptations and doubts'; Dod's 'sins came upon him like armed men'– he 'betook himself to great humiliation' and 'yet for some time he could find no comfort'; Welsh repented as indeed a miserable sinner; Rothwell 'was in a miserable condition of nature' and 'lay for a long time' under 'the spirit of bondage'; Baines was shown 'the evil of his ways,' which led to his repentance; Blackerby 'lay some years in great distress of conscience and much perplexity of spirit'; Bolton was terrified at 'the ugly visage of his sins which lay so heavy upon him' and was attacked by 'foul temptations', which 'continued for many months'; Cotton 'saw his own condition fully discovered' as being 'destitute of true grace' and 'lay for a long time in an uncomfortable despairing way'; Goodwin 'was troubled in conscience for his sins'; Baxter writes, 'it pleased God to awaken my soul, and shew me the folly of sinning . . . many a day I went with a throbbing conscience'; Fox wandered about the country for four years seeking soul satisfaction, fasting much, 'often under great temptations', sometimes in despair, usually miserable, consulting ministers of religion who were unable to satisfy him; Gifford was 'brought to a deep sense of his sins' and 'laboured for about a month' under 'painful convictions'; Bunyan 'became deeply convicted of sin' and alternated between continuing in sin and 'outward reformation'; Fraser left off his former sins and observed religious duties strictly as 'a formal Pharisee', but was then for three years uncertain 'in a waiting and seeking condition'; Tregosse spent some five weeks oscillating between fear and hope as he contemplated his former sins, concluding that all his ministry in the past had been only formal and hypocritical; Broderick and Wilmot were very evident sinners, but both repented sincerely.

2   The Conversion Crisis

ON HIS first reading in Erasmus' version of the New Testament, Bilney 'chanced upon' one sentence, 1 Timothy i. 15, which at once transformed him from 'being almost in despair' to feeling 'a marvellous comfort and quietness'. Later he became acutely conscious that in this discovery of the free forgiveness of his sins he had been led by 'the providence of God'.

Frith's conversion was due mainly to Tyndale, Latimer's to Stafford and Bilney, Hamilton's to Lutheran works, Forret's to a volume written by St. Augustine of Hippo, Straiton's to the conversation of John Erskine, Laird of Dun, Hooper's to the works of Zwingli and Bullinger, Bradford's partly to friendship with Sampson, while for all these converts from Rome a principal factor was their close examination of the contents of the Scriptures. The same anxious comparison between medieval practices and New Testament teaching resulted in the gradual change effected in Gilpin, Chaderton and Hildersam, the last-named being greatly influenced by his schoolmaster at Saffron Walden and his tutor at Cambridge.

The crux of Dod's spiritual development came when 'the Lord sealed to him, that his sins were washed away with the blood of Christ'; Perkins' conversion was initiated by a crisis, when he realised that his drunkenness was 'a by-word among the people'; Welsh sought and found his father's pardon; Midgley was the agent in Rothwell's conversion, Baines in that of Sibbes, Sibbes in that of Cotton, Cotton in that of Preston, Slader in that of Winter, Bruce in that of Henderson; Blackerby's crisis came unexpectedly while 'riding alone' in a sudden illumination, giving him peace of mind after long 'bemoaning his sad condition' Mather's change was brought about through watching the behaviour of Aspinwall, hearing a sermon by Harrison and reading a book by Perkins.

Goodwin's story is notable for his vivid sense of the power of God – his crisis followed at once on hearing Bainbrigge's sermon – but it is God's action, God's grace, God's work, which he emphasises, while he is passive, responsive and compliant; Fox hears a voice telling him, 'There is one, even Christ Jesus, that can speak to thy condition'; he comments on his experience –'the Lord did gently lead me along';[1] Hale's moment of decision comes when one of his companions 'fell down as dead' after drinking far too much; while the Countess of Warwick experienced a slow gradual conversion, caused by the kindness of her father-in-law, by 'afflictions and retirement', by hearing sermons and by 'Christian conference'.

Baxter was deeply impressed by reading works by Bunny, Sibbes and Perkins – he did not know precisely at what point his conversion was effected; Gifford's crisis was sudden, following a loss of money and the perusal of a book by Bolton; Janeway was converted by the life and conversation of an undergraduate, assisted by hearing sermons by Arrowsmith and Hill and reading a work by Baxter.

Bunyan had a most protracted transition, which included more than one crisis – there was first the sudden shock of meeting the few poor women at Bedford, who had an experience which he did not possess but desired to have; then he studied 'the Bible with new eyes', met Gifford, and was helped by

[1]Cf. L. W. Lang, A Study of Conversion (1931), pp. 179–184.

Luther's *Commentary on Galatians*, which showed him that he should 'anchor his faith in a work completed for him long ago';[1] yet he continued oscillating between hope and depression, introspectively examining his feelings, depending on whether he happens to think either of comforting or of denunciatory texts; finally he came to rely on the righteousness of Christ as his own. In all this, he is very conscious of the guidance of God – 'the Lord did work the gracious work of conversion upon my soul.'[2]

That same emphasis occurs also in Fraser's autobiography – 'the Lord, while I was like the prodigal son a great way off, ran to meet me.' His experience is closely similar to that of Simeon in 1779 in being intimately linked with an attendance at the Holy Communion in a University. It is also remarkable for a vision, which resolved his crisis.

Sarah Howley, as a young child, was exceedingly sensitive and devout, but was frightened by alarming passages of Scripture and the preaching about original sin, hell and destruction. She was rescued from these fears by other portions of Scripture and some good books, as well as by more sermons which she approved.

Tregosse dated his conversion from a day when he read an extract 'in an English Divine, touching the greatness and freeness of Christ's love and purchase'; after his repentance, Wilmot's crisis was intellectual – he needed to be convinced of the truth of the Christian faith, and of this he was in a short time fully satisfied.

---

[1] J. Stalker, *John Bunyan*, in *Studies in Conversion* in *The Expositor* (June, 1911), pp. 557-558.

[2] Cf. L. W. Lang, *A Study of Conversion* (1931), pp. 142-149; W. James, *The Varieties of Religious Experience* (1925 ed.), pp. 186-187; T. B. Macaulay, *John Bunyan* (1854), in *Miscellaneous Essays* (1910 ed), pp. 196-200.

3   Post-Conversion

PERMANENCE

HAVING PASSED through a conversion crisis, all the individuals under review felt its effects as permanent, but they did not necessarily in every case reach at once final certainty or peace. Bilney, it is true, when in danger of his life, did recant, but later he bitterly regretted doing so, boldly preached again and suffered burning for his faith. The permanence of their change was likewise exemplified in the martyrdoms of seven others of the thirty-six. Rothwell is an instance of one who, though never losing his assurance, was yet 'subject to many temptations'. Bunyan had temptations to doubt, but they were resolved fairly quickly. Fox, in his highly emotional condition, had periods of acute depression, but his conviction that he was guided by the inner light lasted throughout his eventful life.

EFFECTS ON CHARACTER AND RELIGION

THE MOST noteworthy effect of passing through a conversion crisis was the desire to point the way to others to a like experience. Bilney converted several; Frith influenced some; Latimer's sermons moved many; Hamilton witnessed at once on his return to Scotland; Forret converted a number; Hooper propagated reformed teaching; Gilpin was called 'the Apostle of the North'; Chaderton, Perkins, Welsh, Baines, Bolton, Goodwin, Baxter and Tregosse were all notable as instruments in the conversion of people; Gifford witnesses immediately after his own conversion; Cotton converted Preston.

Bilney and Latimer visited the sick and prisoners; Forret laboured devotedly among the sick and poor in his parish; Bradford sold many possessions to give relief to the poor or sick and incurred the displeasure of his former employer over a matter of restitution and a considerable loss financially; Rothwell was able to comfort many by reason of his own experience of temptation; Hale and Broderick developed noble characters and became splendid examples of Christian laymen; and the Countess of Warwick was famous for her kindness and generosity.

THE ULTIMATE GOAL

IT IS very evident that these experients of conversion did not regard that great episode in their lives as a final end in itself, but as the turning-point towards a life of greater effectiveness. Perhaps Forret, Bradford, Gilpin, Baines, Hildersam, Blackerby, Hale, Fox, the Countess of Warwick, Bunyan and Broderick might be singled out as especially noted for their piety, but they all strove to live holy and useful lives.

4   Special Features

TYPES OF CONVERSION

THE THIRTY-SIX examples of conversion selected here are very far from being repetitive. There is no uniformity in the experiences. Nor can they be rigidly divided into types. Yet some of their differences may be grouped. The first eleven involved a change from medieval thinking and allegiance to Rome to an acceptance of the Reformation and the ideas of its leaders, the transformation including deep religious emotions as well as intellectual satisfaction. Only a few of the later stories are greatly concerned with a denominational issue at the time of conversion, though

Bunyan and Fox, being displeased with the Church of England as they found it, became respectively a Baptist and the founder of the Society of Friends. Henderson transferred his loyalty from the episcopal to the presbyterian system, but the centre of that move was moral rather than doctrinal or institutional. It was a moral dividing line which determined the conversion of most of the others, though the Countess of Warwick found the mental background of the members of her new home daunting, and with Fox and Bunyan the principal characteristic is emotional. The Earl of Rochester required first a moral revolution, then an intellectual convincement. All the chosen instances became ministers of religion, of a wide variety of denominations, except for Hamilton, Straiton, Hale, Broderick, Wilmot, Sarah Howley and the Countess of Warwick.

The reading of Scripture played a large part in the conversions of many of the thirty-six, the other main influences being the example and conversation of friends and acquaintances, the reading of books and the hearing of sermons. With these aids, and with various shocks (as with Straiton, Dod, Perkins, Welsh, Hale, Gifford, Goodwin, Henderson and Wilmot) and illuminations (as with Blackerby and Fox), they may all be said to have been primarily individual rather than corporate in character. They were not the products of mass revivals, though it is true that they took place when the spirit of the age was mostly favourable and such happenings were not entirely unfamiliar or unexpected.

Can these conversions be classified as either sudden or gradual? In even the most catastrophic types of that experience there is probably a considerable period of preparation, even if quite unconscious, also a period of adjustment after the crisis. However, crises themselves vary from the long drawn out to the rapid. This last sort predominates in the stories of Bilney, Latimer, Forret, Straiton, Dod, Perkins, Welsh, Rothwell, Blackerby, Preston, Henderson, Goodwin, Hale, Fox, Gifford and Fraser. As has been well said, 'Conversion may be said to consist in the seeking and the finding of the Saviour. Both of these may synchronize or nearly so; but they may be separated by a wide interval . . . and the interval may be one of pain and even agony'.[1]

VISIONS, DREAMS, AND VOICES

BLACKERBY WHEN alone and in a state of dejection was suddenly and unexpectedly the recipient of a revelation which gave him from that moment peace of mind which lasted to the end of his life. Fox 'heard a voice, which said, "There is one, even Christ Jesus, that can speak to thy condition"' and remained peculiarly sensitive to moments of illumination. Bunyan writes, 'a voice did suddenly dart from Heaven into my soul', and records that years earlier he had when a child been terrified by dreams and visions. Fraser rejoices that 'a marvellous light shined on my understanding.'

THE INFLUENCE OF SEX

IT WOULD be absurd to assert that sex had no impact upon the conversion experiences of any of the thirty-six, but it can be said that there appears to be no positive evidence that it had, and it seems clear that

---

[1] J. Stalker, in *The Expositor* (June, 1911), p. 549.

all these cases of conversion can be accounted for without that influence playing any significant part.

THE AGE OF CONVERSION

THE YEAR of birth of Forret, Straiton and Gifford is unknown, so those three must be omitted here. Some of the others are doubtful, but the estimates given are in all probability not far wrong both as to birth and as to the time of conversion. Of the thirty-three, three were under fifteen years of age (Sarah Howley, Winter and Hildersam), two about fifteen (Welsh and Baxter), three about eighteen (Mather, Janeway and Fraser), ten about twenty to twenty-four (Frith, Baines, Goodwin, Hale, Cotton, Bilney, Hamilton, Blackerby, Fox and Perkins), six about twenty-five to twenty-nine (Preston, Countess of Warwick, Bunyan, Dod, Rothwell and Chaderton), five about thirty to thirty-five (Bolton, Tregosse, Henderson, Wilmot and Latimer), one about thirty-seven (Bradford), two about forty-five (Hooper and Gilpin), and one about fifty-two (Broderick).

CONSCIOUS AND UNCONSCIOUS ELEMENTS

THE ELEMENT of conscious search for religious satisfaction is particularly evident in Hamilton, Hooper, Gilpin, Chaderton, Fox and Bunyan. Bilney exhibits a keen conscious striving, together with an unconscious dissatisfaction with his religious observances. Latimer's oration against Melanchthon was clearly an unconscious preparation for his conversion. Partly unconscious disapprobation of his own behaviour or effectiveness played a part in the crises of Perkins, Bolton, Goodwin, Cotton, Mather, Henderson and

103

Tregosse. Fraser resembles Bilney in endeavouring to keep the whole law and in finding his efforts failing to supply his need.

REVIVALISM

THE PREACHING and writing of some of the thirty-six (Chaderton, Welsh, Perkins, Bolton, and especially Baxter) led to the conversions not only of individuals but also of large numbers. But the most outstanding mass revival of this period occurred in Scotland, at Irvine and Stewarton, Ayrshire (1623 – 1630) under David Dickson, and at Kirk of Shotts, Lanarkshire (1630) under John Livingstone, one of whose sermons was said to gain 500 converts.[1]

[1]T. McCrie, *Sketches of Scottish Church History* (1843), pp. 193–201.

THE RELATION OF
THE CONVERSION EXPERIENCE,

TOGETHER WITH ITS ANTECEDENTS AND ITS AFTER-EFFECTS,

TO DOCTRINAL BELIEF

A REVOLUTION in doctrinal opinions was naturally central in the conversion of the first eleven subjects of this study from Romanism to Protestantism; and the essence of this profound change was joyful acceptance of the doctrine of Justification by Faith with its assurance of forgiveness of sins.

Bilney's reading of one sentence in the New Testament, expounding the need to trust in Christ for salvation, inaugurated his transformation from painful travails, watchings and fastings, 'the redemption of masses and pardons', in a condition of acute anxiety, to a conviction of having been forgiven and 'a marvellous comfort and quietness'. Latimer had been 'as obstinate a papist as any was in England', but on his conversion he 'forsook the school-doctors and such fooleries'; he says that 'all the papists think themselves to be saved by the law', an opinion which he had formerly held but had now come to reject. Frith and Hamilton were largely moulded by Lutheran teaching, Hooper by that of Zwingli and Bullinger. Gilpin took years over carefully weighing the pros. and cons. of the alternatives, and eventually concluded that the decisions of the Council of Trent made it finally impossible for him to accept the authority of Rome. Chaderton also slowly and prayerfully 'examined the points in dispute' and 'decided in favour of the Reformers'. Hildersam, though 'brought up in the Popish manner', accepted the teaching of his schoolmaster, 'a godly man and a religious Protestant', who worked 'in him a liking and relish of the Reformed Religion', and of his similarly-minded tutor at Cambridge.

Most of the remainder of the subjects of this study were educated in a generally Puritan environment, some of them having keenly religious parents, but they all had to appropriate to themselves the truths of the Gospel. With most of them the struggles which led to conversion were chiefly of a moral nature, but with a few the doctrinal aspect was prominent. Happy realisation of free forgiveness of sins is a major element in nearly all these conversion experiences. Baxter's narrative is interesting in showing that he 'knew that Christ was the only mediator by whom we must have pardon, justification, and life' some time before he acquired a 'lively sense of the love of God in Christ to the world or me' or felt that he had 'any special need of him'. The Earl of Rochester, after his moral conversion, needed to be convinced step by step of the truth of Christian doctrine by Burnet and Parsons. But the most remarkable instance of a doctrinal character appears with poor little Sarah Howley, who is terrified by sermons which stressed the doctrine of original sin, the condition of the human race 'by nature' and her own imminent danger of perishing in 'everlasting flames'. It is, however, a relief to be told that she 'died in the full assurance of God's love'. But what is important to notice is that the little book, A Token for Children, records her story and those of twelve other children as meritorious examples of child development, that it was extremely popular, and that it ran to many editions.

Some of those whose stories have been here related, as also other kindred spirits, have written on the subject of conversion. We have already seen Perkins' statement in 1597, and observed the extent of Baxter's works on the subject between 1657 and 1669. Before that, in his most famous book, *The Saints' Everlasting Rest* (1650), he wrote:[1] 'This spiritual regeneration then, is the first and great qualification of these "people of God" . . . There is a two-fold error very common in the descriptions of the work of conversion. The one, of those who only mention the sinner's turning from sin to God, without mentioning any receiving of Christ by faith. The other, of those who on the contrary only mention a sinner's believing, and then think they have said all'.

[handwritten margin note: It's the English ministers who dictate what is to be said]

Bolton defines conversion[2] as 'that holy and happy change wrought upon us by the effectual concurrence of the outward ministry of the Word, and inward working of the Spirit; whereby of natural, carnal, and profane men, we are made spiritual, holy, and new creatures; and from the dominion of sin and Satan, are translated into the kingdom of grace, and into the light and liberty of God's children'. He also asserts[3] that 'a new-born babe in Christ is thoroughly and universally changed; though not yet a perfect man in Christ'.

Goodwin says[4]: 'There are two sorts of conversion of people usual in the church'; that of some 'is accompanied with a mighty, violent inundation of humiliation for sin, and joy and love'; that of others is

---

[1] *Op. cit.* (1887 ed.), Vol. 1, pp. 97–98, 104–105.
[2] Ed. J. Wesley, *A Christian Library*, Vol. 5 (1819), p. 189. From *A Treatise on Self-Examination* (I Cor. xi. 28).
[3] *Ibid.*, Vol. 4 (1819), p. 399. From *On Walking with God* (Genesis vi. 8, 9).
[4] *Ibid.*, Vol. 7 (1820); *cf.* T. Goodwin, *Works*, Vol. 3 (1861), pp. 461–462.

more 'still and quiet . . . their change from darkness to light hath been but as the breaking forth of the morning'. Of these two sorts, 'neither should rejoice against the other, or be discontented with that way, wherein God hath dealt with them'.

Isaac Ambrose (1604 – 1663), a graduate of Brasenose College, Oxford, and afterwards incorporated at Cambridge, was at one time Vicar of Castleton, Derbyshire, and later Vicar of Preston, Lancashire, but was among those ejected for nonconformity in 1662. Some of his sermons were published.[1] He wrote: 'Lo here those steps that raise up a man to the state of regeneration, a sight of sin, sense of misery, sorrow for sin, seeking for comfort, a sight of Christ, desire after Christ, relying on Christ, obedience to Christ.'[2]

Joseph Alleine (1634 – 1668) was recorded as 'setting forth in the Christian race' in 1645, the year in which his elder brother, a clergyman, died, and at the time when he besought his father to have him educated so that he might take his brother's place in the ministry. He took his B.D. degree at Oxford in 1653 and was an assistant minister at Taunton, whence he was ejected for nonconformity in 1662. His book, *An Alarm to Unconverted Sinners*, which enjoyed an immense circulation, was published posthumously in 1672.[3] Defining the nature of conversion, the headings, which he amplifies, are, 'Negatively, 1. It is not the taking on us of the profession of Christianity. 2. It is not the being washed in the laver of regeneration, or putting on the badge of Christ in baptism. 3. It lies not in a merely moral righteousness. 4. It consists not in external

[1]*D.N.B.*
[2]Ed. J. Wesley, *A Christian Library*, Vol. 7 (1820), p. 336. From *The Doctrine of Regeneration* (St. John iii. 3).   [3]*D.N.B.*

conformity to the rules of piety. 5. It lies not in the chaining up of corruption, by education, human laws, or the force of incumbent affliction. It consists not in conviction, in a superficial change, or partial reformation. Positively, it lies in the thorough change both of the heart and life. 1. The author of it is the Spirit of God. 2. The moving cause is internal, or external. (*a*) The internal mover is only free grace. (*b*) The external mover is the merit and intercession of the blessed Jesus. 3. The instrument is either personal or real. (*a*) The personal instrument is the ministry. (*b*) The real instrument is the Word. 4. The final cause is man's salvation, and God's glory. 5. The subject is the sinner, in all his parts and powers, members and mind. Conversion goes (*a*) Throughout the mind. (*b*) Throughout the members. (*c*) Throughout the life and practice. 6. The terms are either from which or to which. (*a*) The terms from which we turn in conversion are sin, Satan, the world, and our own righteousness. (*b*) The terms to which we turn in conversion are either ultimate or subordinate. The ultimate is God the Father, Son, and Holy Ghost, whom the true convert takes as his all-sufficient and eternal blessedness. The mediate term of conversion is either principal, or less principal. The principal is Christ, the only mediator between God and man. The less principal term of conversion is the laws, ordinances, and ways of Christ.' Alleine continues with chapters, 'Of the necessity of conversion; Showing the marks of the unconverted; Showing the miseries of the unconverted; Containing the motives to conversion.'

John Wesley (*c.* 1636 – 1670), grandfather of the founder of the Methodist Societies, a graduate of

Oxford and Vicar of Winterbourne Whitchurch, was another of those who were ejected in 1662 for non conformity.[1] About a year earlier, he had had a conversation with the Bishop of Bristol (Gilbert Ironside), in the course of which he claimed of his ministry: 'It pleased God to seal my labour with success in the apparent conversion of many souls' and that their transformation was 'to the power of godliness, from ignorance and profaneness'; he added that if the bishop would 'lay down any evidences of godliness, agreeing with Scripture, and that are not found in those persons', he would be 'content to be discharged the ministry', for they were indeed converted 'to the reality of religion'. A copy of the record of this conversation, which Wesley describes as 'a remarkable anecdote put into my hands', was inserted by him in his own *Journal* on May 25, 1765.[2]

There is another most important link with the Methodist leader, for in 1750 he published in 50 volumes the first edition of *A Christian Library, consisting of extracts from and abridgments of the choicest pieces of practical divinity, which have been published in the English tongue*. This work which was re-issued in 30 volumes (1819 – 1827), covered a very wide range, and many of the extracts were preceded by short lives of the authors or of their subjects. In this way, eighteenth and nineteenth century Methodist readers would have been made familiar with the conversions of Bilney, Frith, Latimer, Hamilton, Straiton, Hooper, Bradford, Gilpin, Welsh, Blackerby, Bolton, Winter, Mather, Hale, and

[1] J. S. Simon, *John Wesley and the Religious Societies* (1921), pp. 31–34.
[2] Ed. N. Curnock, *The Journal of the Reverend John Wesley*, Standard Edition, (1909), Vol. 5, pp. 119–124; cf. E. Calamy, revised S. Palmer, *The Nonconformist's Memorial* (2nd ed. 1777), Vol. 1, p. 481.

Fraser, though some of their stories are given only very brief treatment. They would also be aware of recent examples resulting from the ministry of Jonathan Edwards in New England, and would have been enabled to study teaching on the subject by Baxter, Bolton, Goodwin, Ambrose and Alleine, also by John Arndt, Blaise Pascal, Hugh Binning, Henry More, Bishop Edward Reynolds and Jonathan Edwards. They would also have had access to many devotional works, including *The Spiritual Bee*, which had appealed to Sarah Howley, and writings by Foxe, Clarke, Preston, Sibbes, Manton, Owen, Bunyan and Scougal.

It is also interesting to notice that of the thirty-six persons, whose conversion narratives have been recorded here, some account of the lives of eighteen appeared in J. Gillies, *Historical Collections relating to the Success of the Gospel* (2 vols. 1754), of twenty in E. Middleton, *Biographia Evangelica* (4 vols. 1779 – 1786), and of fourteen in B. Brook, *Lives of the Puritans* (3 vols. 1813), only seven appearing in none of these works.

By no means all of those whose deeply-felt and wholly sincere religion was of the Puritan or Evangelical kind passed through a conscious crisis of conversion. John Milton was one who did not do so.[1] Another notable instance is that of John Livingstone (1603 – 1672), whose ministry converted crowds, yet who stated that he had himself no recollection of any specific time of conversion.[2] Other examples would seem to include Thomas Hill (*d.* 1653),[3] Owen Stockton

---

[1] S. T. Coleridge, *Essays and Lectures* (Everyman's Library ed. 1907), p. 282.
[2] *Autobiography* (1666), in Ed. W. K. Tweedie, *Select Biographies*, Vol. 1 (1845). pp. 130–132.
[3] Ed. S. Clarke, *The Lives of Thirty-Two English Divines* (1677), p. 230.

(1630 – 1680),[1] Matthew Henry (1662 – 1714),[2] his sister Mrs. Sarah Savage (born 1664),[3] and Isaac Watts (1674 – 1748),[4] The same is true of Henry Scougal (1650 – 1678),[5] the author of *The Life of God in the Soul of Man* (1677), a work which played a part in the conversion of George Whitefield,[6] but as he was a Scottish Episcopalian a spiritual growth without a crisis would be more normal. We find therefore variety in the doctrinal approach to the idea of a conversion involving a definite crisis, but there was unanimity in the acceptance of the doctrine of Justification by Faith, the glad expression of thankfulness to and trust in Christ, whose sacrifice sufficed for the forgiveness of sins of all who believed; it was also generally agreed that the activity of the Holy Spirit was the initial foundation and cause of the regeneration of a man, and that God's grace was indispensable.

---

[1]Ed. S. Clarke, *The Lives of Sundry Eminent Persons* (1683), Part 1, pp. 186–187.
[2]*Dictionary of National Biography.*   [3]J. B. Williams, *Memoirs* (1829), pp. 1–5.
[4]T. Gibbons, *Memoirs of Isaac Watts* (1780); D.N.B.
[5]G. Burnet, *Life of Scougal* (1739 ed.).
[6]F. W. B. Bullock, *Evangelical Conversion in Great Britain, 1696–1845* (1959), pp. 28–30, 197, 201.

THE VALUE OF
THE EXPERIENCE OF CONVERSION

WHAT IS the value of the conversion experience? We have seen that the effects upon character and religion of our selected experients of a conversion were very great. The results were permanent, though not always completed quickly; their moral and spiritual attitudes were totally changed; not end products, these conversions through a short or long period of crisis were turning-points in their lives, leading on to a usefulness and holiness which they would not have otherwise achieved. The fruit of a good life is the authentic test of value.

But is a conversion necessary for everybody? The answer depends upon the use made of the word 'conversion'. If it be interpreted literally and naturally as meaning a conscious turning round, whether apparently sudden or gradual, involving of necessity some pivotal point of crisis, at which a change is inaugurated, then the value of that experience is unquestionable, as is evident in many persons' lives. But such a happening is far from being universal in the spiritual development of multitudes of the most godly men and women of Christian history. There are, however, some writers who use the word 'conversion' in a much wider and more general sense, not requiring any specific crisis or turning-point, but including after baptism the process of growth by education and training, a quiet gradual acceptance of commitment and discipleship. If 'conversion' can be stretched to include such all-embracing types of Christian attachment and decision, then assuredly conversion is essential for all. But it would seem more reasonable to interpret the word 'con-version' to mean a radical change brought about through some storm and stress, a crisis, and a happy release to newness of life; in which case, it is the necessary experience for some people, but not the route for all, for there are many ways of finding God, many avenues to holiness of life, many gates to the heavenly city. The Spirit of God works upon a multiplicity of human souls, for whose varying needs no uniform treatment could suffice.[1]

---

[1]See further, F. W. B. Bullock, *Evangelical Conversion in Great Britain, 1696–1845* (1959), pp. 4–7, 270–280; J. Baillie, *Baptism and Conversion* (1964), pp. 104–112.

ADDENDA to

EVANGELICAL CONVERSION

IN GREAT BRITAIN, 1696 – 1845

To page 3. Note 5. Among the conversion stories of various countries and periods, note that of Joachim Neander (1640 – 1680) (*cf.* C. Winkworth, *Christian Singers of Germany*, 1869, pp. 284–288); while J. J. Moser in 1733–1735 made a collection of conversion narratives (*cf.* A. L. Drummond, *German Protestantism since Luther*, 1951, p. 76). On Zwingli's attitude, *cf.* J. A. Dorner, *History of Protestant Theology*, Vol. 1 (1871), pp. 290–291. The 'sudden conversion' of Calvin was told by himself (*cf.* M. Guizot, *St. Louis and Calvin*, 1878, pp. 158–159). On the gradual change in Bullinger and his father, see his *Decades* (Parker Society), Vol. 5 (1852), pp. vii–x. Some recent conversions of varying kinds may be studied in: Ed. J. A. Pike, *Modern Canterbury Pilgrims* (1956); Ed. D. Morgan, *They Became Anglicans* (1959); Ed. D. Morgan, *They Became Christians* (1966); H. W. Yoxall, *Journey into Faith*; and A. E. Gould, *Changed Men of Our Time*. See also *Memorials of Captain Hedley Vicars* (1856); A. E. Reffold, *Wilson Carlile and the Church Army* (5th ed. 1956), pp. 26–30; C. F. Andrews, *What I owe to Christ* (1932), Chapter 5; and G. F. Dempster, *Finding Men for Christ*. A dramatically sudden conversion in Rome in the early years of the fourth century from paganism to Christianity is that of St. Genesius. Some striking conversion stories from the twelfth century appear in J. C. Morison, *The Life and Times of St. Bernard* (ed. of 1868), pp. 12–15, 194–196.

To page 9. In his *Journal*, John Wesley recorded several other examples of piety, dating back to a time before his own evangelical conversion, as follows:—

On December 5, 1738, he mentions the conversion of W. F. about 1720.

On May 19, 1752, he says that Mrs. Armstrong, 'fourscore years of age' had loved the oracles of God 'from a child'—say, from about 1680.

On April 18, 1757, he refers to one who 'had Christ clearly revealed to him thirty years ago'– c.1727.

On July 18, 1759, he observed one, 'who had known the Lord above five and twenty years'– since c.1733.

On June 18, 1766, he met one who 'was justified thirty years ago, and another of them two and forty' – i.e. in 1736 and 1724.

On March 18, 1781, he writes of 'Mr. Arthur Bedford', incumbent of the Temple Church, Bristol, 'a person greatly esteemed fifty or sixty years ago for piety as well as learning'– that is, c.1721–1731. J. S. Simon, *John Wesley and the Religious Societies* (1921) says that Mr. Bedford was active there as early as 1709.

For a notice in the *Journal* of September 14, 1751, referring back to the year 1695, see above, *Preface*. A fine testimony to piety found amongst many poor people was given by William Law, in *A Serious Call to a Devout and Holy Life* (1729), Chapter 19 – p. 216 in ed. of 1888.

On some other evangelical trends in the first quarter of the eighteenth century, see C. Hole, *A Manual of English Church History* (1910), pp. 347–349.

To page 258, note 4. Add, *cf.* C. Hole, *A Manual of English Church History* (1910), pp. 390–391, 410, 418–419.

INDEX

ALESS, A. 6
Alleine, J. 108, 111
Ambrose, I. 108, 111
Aquinas, T. 7
Arndt, J. 111
Arrowsmith, Dr. 71, 97
Arthur, T. 2
Aspinwall, E. 48, 97
Augustine, St. 2, 13, 96

BAINBRIGGE, T. 54, 97
Baines, P. 38-39, 91, 93, 95, 96, 99, 100, 103
Barnes, R. 2
Barrowe, H. ix
Baxter, R. x, 32, 59-62, 71, 91, 92, 94, 95, 97, 99, 103, 104, 106, 107, 111
Bayly, L. 73, 77, 94
Beaton, D. 14
Beaton, J. 11
Bilney, T. 1-3, 8-10, 91, 92, 94, 96, 99, 102, 103, 104, 105, 110
Binning, H. 111
Blackerby, R. 32, 40-41, 91, 92, 93, 95, 96, 100, 101, 102, 103, 110
Bolton, R. 42-43, 69, 92, 93, 95, 97, 99, 103, 104, 107, 110, 111
Bradford, J. 19-20, 91, 92, 96, 100, 103, 110
Broderick, Sir A. viii, 85-86, 92, 93, 95, 100, 101, 103
Brook, B. 111
Bruce, R. 52-53, 96
Bucer, M. 19
Bugenhagen, J. 12
Bullinger, H. 17, 18, 96, 105
Bunny, E. 60, 97
Bunyan, J. viii, 73-76, 94, 95, 97, 99, 100, 101, 102, 103, 111
Burnet, G. 87-89, 106

CALDERWOOD, D. 15
Chaderton, L. 26-27, 46, 91, 92, 93, 96, 99, 103, 104, 105
Chaderton, T. 26-27
Charlton, M. x
Chester, A. G. 7
Clarke, S. 36, 111
Colet, J. 4
Corrie, G. E. 8
Cotton, J. 32, 44-45, 46-47, 91, 94, 95, 96, 99, 103
Cranmer, T. 5, 7.
Cromwell, O. x, 56

DEMAUS, R. 7
Dent, A. 73
Dickson, D. 35, 104
Dod, J. 30-31, 47, 91, 93, 94, 96, 101, 102, 103

EDWARDS, J. 111
Erasmus, D. 1, 2-3, 11, 21, 96
Erskine, J. 15-16, 96

FORRET, T. 13-14, 92, 96, 99, 100, 102, 103
Forsyth, A. 34-35
Fox, G. viii, 63-65, 91, 94, 95, 97, 100, 101, 102, 103
Foxe, J. 6, 9-10, 15, 111
Fraser, J. 77-79, 94, 95, 98, 102, 103, 104, 111
Frith, J. 4-6, 92, 96, 99, 103, 105, 110

GIFFORD, J. viii, 69-70, 74, 93, 95, 97, 99, 101, 102, 103
Gillies, J. 111
Gilpin, B. 6, 21-25, 92, 93, 94, 96, 99, 100, 103, 105, 110
Gladstanes, G. 52
Goodwin, T. 47, 54-56, 91, 92, 94, 95, 97, 99, 101, 102, 103, 107, 111
Gourlay, N. 15
Gower, S. 36

HALE, SIR M. 57-58, 91, 92, 94, 97, 100, 101, 102, 103, 110
Hamilton, P. 5, 6, 11-12, 92, 96, 99, 101, 103, 105, 110
Harrington, Sir J. 19, 20
Harrison, Mr. 48, 97
Henderson, A. 52-53, 92, 94, 96, 101, 102, 103
Henry, M. 112
Hildersam, A. 28-29, 47, 91, 92, 93, 96, 100, 103, 105
Hill, T. 71, 97, 111
Hooper J. 17-18, 92, 96, 99, 103, 105, 110
Howley, S. viii, 80-82, 98, 101, 103, 106, 111
Howley, W. 80

IRONSIDE, G. 110

117